The New
SOUTHERN
BASICS

The New SOUTHERN BASICS

Traditional Southern Food for Today

MARTHA PHELPS STAMPS

A CUMBERLAND HOUSE HEARTHSIDE BOOK

CUMBERLAND HOUSE
Nashville, Tennessee

Published by Cumberland House Publishing, Inc.
431 Harding Industrial Drive
Nashville, Tennessee 37211

Design by Bruce Gore, Gore Studio, Inc., Nashville, Tennessee.
Art by Donna Glassford.

Library of Congress Cataloging-in-Publication Data

Stamps, Martha, 1961–
    The new southern basics / Martha Stamps.
        p. cm.
    Includes index.
    ISBN 1-888952-26-1 (alk. paper)
    1. Cookery, American—Southern style.   I. Title.
TX715.2.S68S8 1997
641.5975—dc21   96-49094
                                                                   CIP

Printed in the United States of America
4 5 6 7 — 05 04 03

To Catherine Couch
and my daughter, Moriah.

Contents

INTRODUCTION   ix

1   THE PANTRY   3

2   SNACKS   11

3   SALADS   23

4   SOUPS   33

5   VEGETABLES AND SIDES   47

6   FRITTERS AND LITTLE FRIED THINGS   103

7   SEAFOOD   109

8   POULTRY   119

9   MEATS   135

10   BREADS   151

11   CAKES, CANDY, AND COOKIES   171

12   PIES AND COBBLERS   195

13   ICE CREAM, PUDDINGS, AND GOOEY STUFF   211

14   BEVERAGES   217

INDEX   221

Introduction

Being southern and being passionate about food are inseparable bricks in my very foundation. My ancestors hunted in Middle Tennessee even before they became a part of the first European settlement founded on the banks of the Cumberland River in 1779. My parents instilled in me a pride in my heritage and a great respect for tradition, a tradition which carried over into what we ate and why. Way before it was back in vogue, my mother baked bread, simmered chickens for stock, and made us cookies from scratch, just as her mother had. My parents are older than most of my friends' parents, and my mother's mother was thirty-nine when Mama was born, almost unheard of in the those days. While I never gave it much thought as a child, I have come to believe that these stretches of age between the generations in my family have added a dimension of personal interest for me in history and my own heritage. My grandmother was born in 1887, the youngest of older parents as well. Her father fought in the Civil War. So stories of "the old days" were not as abstract to me as they are to most kids. They were stories about people I actually knew and loved. One of these people I loved who dearly loved food was my grandmother, Anna Martha Cooper Frost. In fact, she actually taught cooking before she married, quite the modern woman. I spent a lot of time in her kitchen as a child, a well ordered kitchen which she controlled quite well. But the soul of the kitchen resided in the person of Catherine Couch, Grandmama's housekeeper. In my earliest memory I am standing on a stool in my grandmother's kitchen "helping" Catherine Couch make fried peach pies. I remember the smell of summer, the steam from the pies, and burning my fingers on the sticky sweet filling. I remember the strength I felt in the shoulders I leaned against as my arms encircled Catherine Couch's neck. I remember her patience and her pride, pride which shone in everything that came out of that kitchen.

Couch took her time and hummed as she worked. She cleaned her own greens and shelled her own peas. There wasn't much in her freezer other than ice. She taught me how to work the shortening into the flour with just my fingertips and to be generous with the pepper, but mainly she taught me to respect the art of cooking and to love the food. To Couch cooking was more than just a job; cooking was an act of art and love.

In our recent history, cooking lost a vital dimension. As lives became more and more hectic, eating became an inconvenience and cooking a chore. Any measure which could render the job of feeding the family more convenient was hallowed. Instant foods, frozen foods, microwaves—these became the indispensable tools of the kitchen, replacing the knowledge and techniques once handed down from generation to generation.

Blessedly, a change is occurring throughout the nation and particularly in the South: a culinary Renaissance, if you will. In a direct reaction against our frantic work schedules, more and more people are becoming passionate about their home lives. Parents and children are sitting down together for dinner, once again desiring mealtime to become the great family forum for bonding and debate, a time to look forward to and linger over. Only now you can bet that there is no housekeeper preparing these meals. Couples are cooking together as an intimate pastime, and children are learning alongside their parents as our generation looks eagerly backwards to less complicated times.

The cuisine that I embrace reaches back to a generation which took the time to do things right. In past times, folks used fresh ingredients because that's all that was available. I like to cook from scratch because everything simply tastes better that way, to say nothing of being enormously more valuable nutritionally and economically as well, especially when local food stuffs are fully utilized. Besides, scratch cooking is much more interesting and loads more fun than opening cans and boxes. The food in these pages celebrates the connection between dirt and farmer, pumpkin and pie, between stream and trout and frying pan. I have always loved the innate rhythms of the kitchen; in shelling peas, cleaning greens and kneading dough, a heart beat reflected in the slow dance of the seasons: in growth, harvest, and sustenance. I believe that our generation, especially in these hectic times, can find comfort in these natural rhythms and cycles that remain in our world.

The South has always made itself the victim of humorous little quips. A favorite of mine is that in Nashville in the sixties, all you needed to be a gourmet cook was a box of Velveeta and a can of mushroom soup. A bit harsh perhaps, but a statement of frighteningly wide spread veracity. Most unfortunately, this "casserole cuisine" has become what too frequently is equated with southern cooking. In fact, true southern food is based on a heritage of skilled cooking with an abundant variety of fresh ingredients.

Many of the latest "new" food trends, such as wild greens and mushrooms, local goat cheese and root vegetable purées are all mainstays of traditional southern cooking, a simple and gutsy cuisine, not unlike the immensely popular peasant cooking of southern Europe.

The desecration of honest southern cooking occurred during the middle of this century for many reasons. The Great Depression and World War II necessitated a move away from domestic help, and sadly, many home makers of the middle and upper classes had simply not been trained to cook. So much of traditional southern cooking is indebted to the thousands of women like Catherine Couch who provided delicious and nurturing nourishment—soul food, if you will—to their employers and families for generations. The void that was left when these women left the kitchens of many white families has really never been filled.

And so you find women like my grandmother teaching cooking and home economics at the beginning of this century to women who probably had grown up thinking they'd never have to know these things. As the course of the twentieth century progressed and more and more women joined the work force, time and ease became the over riding factors in home cooking.

In a related manner, the disappearance of the family kitchen garden coincided with the wide spread use of frozen vegetables and giant grocery chains, rendering a dismal homogeneous character to the foods we ate. Whereas cook books written before the depression list a staggering array of local vegetables and fruits, later cookbooks show that list growing shorter and shorter, as people became limited to what was available on the grocery store shelves and freezers. Until very recently, way too many of the "exotic" or sophisticated European ingredients that have trickled into widespread use, apparently replacing traditional ingredients, arrived on our grocery shelves dried, stale, and tasteless.

The southern food that I cook celebrates a return to foods of character. Call me a purist. I like to know all of the ingredients that go into the foods that I prepare.

Fresh fried trout with stone ground corn meal crust, tomato sandwiches with garlicky home made mayonnaise, spicy gingerbread made with sorghum molasses: this is the southern food which has found its way to the hottest restaurants in New York and Los Angeles, but which tastes even better at home. This is food to get exited about. This stuff is worth taking a little time and giving a little effort, for your friends, your family, your own satisfaction.

Today, people across the country are searching the past, looking back for a different lifestyle, a slower pace, a higher quality in everything that surrounds them. What we eat and why is so embedded into our culture, it's hard to know which affects which. To quote a booklet published by a small dairy farm in upstate New York: "In twenty-first century culinary history texts, the twentieth century will be characterized as the Century of Quantity's triumph over Quality. We ... are proud to be among the harbingers of the end of that century." This is really more than food that we are talking about. These are issues of idealism and integrity.

Like the owners of that dairy, I am passionate about what I eat, where it comes from, how I cook it, and even the setting in which I eat it. I want to share that passion, to sing about it, really. But mostly I want to share the wonderful feeling of making something you are proud of, and giving it to the pleasure and nourishment of someone you love. That is my greatest passion.

❧

I would like to thank Jim Knowles and John Sanders for implementing this project; Donna Glassford for her beautiful vision; my precious friends for their patience, support and wit; and Mama, Daddy, Sallie, and Mary for feeding me enough love to conquer any challenge.

The New
SOUTHERN
BASICS

Chapter 1

THE PANTRY

The Southern pantry was much more than a dark room off to the side of the kitchen. The pantry served as a vital organ in that kitchen. It was a year round flavor connection to summer, the storehouse of fruits and vegetables picked at their peak. Furthermore, pantry pickles and relishes provided a great deal of the flavor in many meals. Lightly seasoned roasts, potatoes, sandwiches, and stews all came alive with the vinegar and spices from the relish tray. A dining room table would have a special relish tray of silver or cut glass with three to five compartments for holding chow chow, bread and butter pickles, and maybe chutney or cranberry sauce. The kitchen table played host to three to five glass jars, their lids removed and a spoon unceremoniously stuck inside. However they were served, pickles and preserves were there at almost every meal, and a bottle of hot sauce, too.

But what we really lost when we stopped "putting up" these things ourselves was a great deal more than flavor. We're missing out on the fellowship and ritual of folks gathered together in the kitchen, working around the table, gossiping, laughing, and sharing each others' lives as well as their recipes. Sure, there are some pretty good pickles and jellies at the grocery store. But those clerks in that store aren't going to tell you what to do about your boyfriend or how to stop your baby's ear aches or why your roses won't bloom. A big chore like preserving is easier when it's a group effort. You'll get the job done quicker, and everytime you taste those peach preserves, you can also taste the smiles and jokes of someone you love.

Ingredients

10	pounds ripe tomatoes
3	sticks cinnamon
2	teaspoons whole cloves
2	tablespoons black pepper-corns
2	pounds green bell peppers
1	pound brown sugar
2	heads garlic, peeled and minced
5	pounds onions, chopped fine
1/2	pound grated fresh horse-radish
1/4	cup salt

CHILI SAUCE

A sweet and sour relish, used on meats and vegetables alike.

MAKES 4 TO 5 QUARTS.

Preparation

Bring a large pot of water to a simmer. Prepare a large bowl with ice water. Core the tomatoes and blanch in batches in simmering water for about 1 minute, until the skin pulls away easily. Remove from the pot and plunge into the ice water. When cool, remove from the ice water, peel, squeezing out as many seeds as you can without making yourself crazy. Place the tomatoes in a heavy pot and cook down for 1 hour, stirring occasionally.

While the tomatoes are cooking, use a coffee grinder or a mortar and pestle to grind the cinnamon sticks, cloves, and peppercorns very fine. Add along with the other ingredients and cook for 2 hours. Taste for seasoning. Pour into sterile jars and process in a water bath to keep indefinitely, or cover and refrigerate for up to 2 weeks.

Ingredients

4	gallons ripe tomatoes
3	onions, chopped
12	cloves garlic, minced
6	cups vinegar
1	cup horseradish
4	bell peppers, chopped
1	tablespoon dry mustard
1	tablespoon celery seed
2	tablespoons black pepper
1	teaspoons red pepper
1/4	cup salt

TOMATO KETCHUP

This is really marvelous. French fries will never be the same!

MAKES 4 TO 5 QUARTS.

Preparation

Blanch the tomatoes in simmering water for about 30 seconds. Place in ice water. Peel and roughly chop. Boil until thick and soft.

Strain through a sieve. There should be 1 gallon of pulp. Place back in the pot and add the remaining ingredients. Boil slowly 1 hour or more until thick, stirring frequently to prevent burning. Bottle and seal while still hot.

CHOW CHOW

A great all around condiment to add flavor to lightly seasoned foods.

MAKES ABOUT 7 PINTS.

Ingredients

- 6 pounds cabbage
- 6 green tomatoes
- 2 large yellow onions
- 3 cayenne peppers
- 1/2 cup salt
- 1/2 pound sugar
- 1 quart vinegar
- 1 tablespoon turmeric
- 1 tablespoon ground ginger
- 1/2 tablespoon celery seed
- 1/2 tablespoon ground cloves
- 1/2 tablespoon ground cinnamon

Preparation

Put the vegetables through a food grinder or chop in a food processor. Stir in the salt. Place in a colander lined with a cheesecloth and let drip for 2 hours.

Add the sugar, vinegar, turmeric, ginger, celery seed, cloves, and cinnamon. Place in a heavy pot and boil together for 20 minutes. Seal in sterile jars.

WATERMELON PICKLE

Sweet and crispy.

MAKES ABOUT 12 PINTS.

Ingredients

- Rind of 1 large watermelon
- Water
- Salt
- 1 ounce cinnamon sticks
- 1 teaspoon whole cloves
- 2 quarts white vinegar
- 1 1/2 pounds light brown sugar

Preparation

Peel the watermelon rind, cut in 1/2-inch thick cubes, and place in a large ceramic bowl. Make a brine of salt and water that is strong enough to float an egg (1 gallon water to 1/2 cup salt). Pour over the rind; let stand overnight. Drain, place in a non-reactive pot, and cover with cold water. Bring to a boil and boil the rind about 30 minutes until tender. Drain and set aside. Boil the spices with the vinegar and sugar. Add the melon and cook until it is clear, about 30 minutes. Pack in sterile jars and process in a water bath.

Ingredients

- 2 dozen cucumbers
  Peeled cloves from 1 head
  garlic
- 2/3 quart white vinegar
- 1/3 quart water
- 1 cup sugar
- 1 1/2 tablespoons whole mustard
  seed
- 1 tablespoon turmeric
- 1 tablespoon celery seed
  Few cinnamon sticks
- 1 teaspoon whole cloves
- 1 teaspoon ground allspice

BREAD AND BUTTER PICKLES

The only sweet cucumber pickle I like. The garlic makes it.

MAKES ABOUT 6 PINTS.

Preparation

Slice the cucumbers and sprinkle lightly with salt. Allow to stand overnight.

Drain in the morning. Boil together the garlic, vinegar, water, and sugar with the spices. Add the cucumbers and boil about 20 minutes until tender. Place in sterilized jars and seal. Process in a water bath.

Ingredients

- About 18 to 20 smallest
  cucumbers, finger size
- 2 large sprigs dill with seeds
- 2 small bay leaves
- 6 fresh cayenne peppers
- 1 quart water
- 1 quart white vinegar

DILL PICKLES

A classic, and very pretty with the dill sprigs.

MAKES 2 1-QUART JARS.

Preparation

Clean the cucumbers and pack in sterile jars, along with 1 sprig of dill, 1 bay leaf, and 3 cayenne peppers per jar. Boil the water with the vinegar and pour over the cucumber. Seal in a hot water bath.

4 pints water

1 pint salt

1 quart chopped green tomatoes (4 medium tomatoes)

1 quart chopped onion (2 onions)

1 cauliflower, divided into florets

4 green bell peppers, diced

4 red bell peppers, diced

4 stalks celery, diced

1 cup all-purpose flour

6 tablespoons dry mustard

1 tablespoon turmeric

1 tablespoon celery seed

1 cup sugar

6 cups white vinegar

1 quart ¼-inch thick cucumber slices (about 4 cucumbers)

MUSTARD PICKLE

Try this with roasted meats like lamb or pork loin.

MAKES ABOUT 12 PINTS.

Preparation

Boil the water with the salt to make a brine and pour over the tomatoes, onion, cauliflower, bell peppers, and celery. Let stand for 24 hours.

Drain and place in a heavy pot. Cover with cold water and bring to a boil. Drain immediately.

Mix the flour, dry mustard, turmeric, celery seed, and sugar together and whisk in the vinegar to make 2 quarts. Place the drained vegetables back in the pot with the cucumber and pour the dressing over. Place on low heat and, stirring frequently, bring to a slight boil. Taste to adjust the seasoning. Pack in jars and process in a water bath.

CABBAGE PICKLE

I eat this right out of the jar. Almost like a cole slaw.

MAKES ABOUT 12 PINTS.

- 3 quarts water
- ³/4 pound salt
- 7 pounds shredded cabbage
- 2 pounds sliced onion
- 6 banana peppers, cut in ¹/2-inch slices
- 2 quarts white vinegar

Preparation

Boil the water with the salt and pour over the cabbage. Cover and let stand overnight.

Drain the cabbage and squeeze as dry as possible. Place the cabbage, onion, and peppers in a pot and pour the vinegar over. Stir and cook for 45 minutes.

Pack in jars and process in a water bath to can indefinitely, or keep covered in the refrigerator for several weeks.

SPICED PEACHES

These are so welcome on the dinner table in the dead of winter, and year round, of course.

MAKES ABOUT 8 PINTS.

Ingredients

- 1 tablespoon allspice
- 2 sticks cinnamon
- 1 teaspoon whole cloves
- 1 teaspoon celery seed
- 1 tablespoon mace
- 1 quart vinegar
- 2 pounds sugar
- 7 pounds peaches, slightly underripe

Preparation

Tie the spices in cheesecloth and cook for 15 minutes with the vinegar and sugar to make a syrup.

Bring a large pot of water to a slow boil and blanch the peaches for about 1 minute, until the peel pulls away. Remove from the pot and drop in ice water. Peel. Cook the peeled peaches a few at a time in the syrup, until they are easily pierced. As the peaches are cooked, split and remove the pit and spread them out on platters until they all are done.

Cook the syrup down until fairly thick and remove the spices. Pack the peaches in sterile jars, pour the syrup over, and process in a water bath.

Ingredients

2½ pounds peaches
½ cup water
1 pound sugar
1 stick cinnamon

PEACH JAM

Summertime in a jar.

MAKES ABOUT 4 HALF-PINTS.

Preparation

Bring a pot of water to boil and drop in the peaches. Cook for 1 to 2 minutes, until the skins slip off. Cut the peaches in 1-inch pieces. Place in a non-reactive saucepan with ½ cup of water and bring to a boil. Boil for 10 minutes.

Add the sugar and cinnamon and boil for 20 minutes, stirring occasionally, until the syrup is thickened and a candy thermometer registers at least 216°. Pour while hot into jars and seal.

Ingredients

6 pounds rhubarb, cut in 1-inch pieces
6 lemons, sliced thin, seeds removed
6 pounds sugar

RHUBARB JAM

This is truly very pretty, with the lemon slices, and has a nice tart taste.

MAKES ABOUT 8 PINTS.

Preparation

Place the rhubarb and lemon in a nonreactive bowl and pour the sugar over. Let stand for 24 hours.

Place in a nonreactive pot and boil for 45 minutes, stirring gently to avoid breaking up the fruit. There should be pieces of fruit and lemon in the finished jam. After 45 minutes, pack in sterile jars and process in a water bath.

BLACKBERRY JAM

Pristine and lip smacking good.

MAKES ABOUT 4 HALF-PINTS.

Ingredients

1   quart blackberries
1/4   cup water
4   cups sugar

Preparation

Rinse and drain the blackberries. Mash slightly. Place in a saucepan with the water. Bring to a boil and cook for 5 minutes until soft. Add the sugar, stir, and heat to 218°, stirring occasionally. Pour while hot into 4 sterile half-pint jars. Seal and process in a water bath.

PEAR AND GINGER CONSERVE

Delicious on toast. This is nice with ham, as well.

MAKES ABOUT 10 PINTS.

Ingredients

8   pounds pear slices (about 10 pounds whole pears)
1/2   pound candied ginger, finely minced
8   pounds sugar
4   lemons, sliced in thin circles and seeded

Preparation

Place the pears, ginger, and sugar in a nonreactive saucepan and boil slowly for 1 hour.

While that is cooking, place the lemons in a small nonreactive saucepan, cover with water, and boil for 30 minutes.

Drain the lemon slices and add to the pears. Boil for 30 more minutes. Pour into sterile jars while hot and seal in a water bath.

Chapter 2

SNACKS

❧

*S*nacks at my grandmother's house were never inconsequential. No bags of Doritoes or cans of dip. Snacks, like the rest of the family's sustenance, were thoughtfully prepared, composed even. While a snack might be casual, it was never mundane. This deliberate essence of snacking had two very positive results. First of all, there was much less compulsive eating. No microwave popcorn to blindly cram into our mouths with our greasy little fists. In fact popcorn itself was a much anticipated treat. On rainy afternoons after school, it could be made on top of the stove in a big pot with a little oil. Remember testing to see how hot the oil was? Grandmama instructed me to use three kernels—no less and no more. Great anticipation and much excitement when you heard the kernels zing, zing, zing against the aluminum lid. The alternate festive option was wire popcorn baskets cooked over an open fire. Campfire popcorn was one of the trappings of a truly exceptional event, a hay ride or possibly an outdoor overnight.

Most snacks were entered into with even greater purpose. Open-face sandwiches were made on white bread rolled out very thin, spread with garlicky homemade mayonnaise and cut out in the perfect size circle to fit the chosen tomato or cucumber slice. A dash of salt and paprika, a crank of the pepper grinder, a garnish of parsley or watercress. Lay these on a silver tray with a doily underneath and carry them to the side porch where folks are enjoying homemade lemonade in tall glasses with thin circles of lemon and sprigs of mint floating on top. That's the way to snack. Listen to bees buzz in the wisteria or maybe the soft thwack of the neighbor's push lawn mower. Have a sandwich and pass the tray. Fall asleep with your head in Mama's lap while the grown-ups talk politics. These were Sunday afternoons at Grandmama's.

The end result of this celebratory snacking is an obvious one. The snacks taste marvelous, to die for. Of course you must take as much time to savor them as it takes to make them. The tomatoes should be slightly warm from the garden. The herbs are best picked just outside the kitchen door. Only make as many sandwiches as you need, for they won't keep well for long. Of course, however many you make will get eaten quickly enough.

COLD CUCUMBER SANDWICHES

Ingredients

1   fresh local cucumber
1/2   cup white wine vinegar
1   teaspoon sugar
6   slices white or whole wheat bread, figuring three circles to a bread slice
1/4   cup homemade mayonnaise
   Salt and white pepper
   Fresh dill sprigs

MAKES ABOUT 18 SMALL SANDWICHES.

Preparation

Score the cucumber with the tines of a fork and slice about 1/8-inch thick circles. Taste a couple of slices to be sure the cucumber is not bitter. Cucumber sizes vary widely and I am broadly approximating 18 slices per cuke. If there are some really small ones, I like to overlap 3 slices per sandwich. Soak the cucumber slices in the vinegar and sugar while preparing the bread. Cut out the bread with a biscuit cutter. White bread will make a more delicate sandwich, but a nutty whole wheat can be quite nice also.

Spread the bread with the mayonnaise. Top with a slice of cucumber (blotted dry), salt, pepper, and dill. Cover with a slightly moist towel or napkin until ready to serve.

OPEN-FACE TOMATO SANDWICHES

MAKES 5 SANDWICHES.

1 perfect tomato, never out of season

5 slices good white bread, preferably homemade

1/4 cup homemade mayonnaise, (Hellman's, if it must be store bought; don't even think about reduced calorie mayo or I'll send the ghost of Grandmother out to haunt you)

Salt to taste

Paprika to taste

Black pepper to taste

Cayenne pepper sparingly, if you like

A sprinkle of fresh herbs (usually parsley or watercress, though basil has become the modern-day choice)

Preparation

Core the tomato and slash an X in the other end. Bring a pot of water to a simmer and drop the tomato in for about 20 seconds, until the peel starts to pull away. Be careful not to leave the tomato in for too long. It will quickly start to cook and get mushy. Use a slotted spoon to scoop the tomato out of the pot and hold it under cool water. The peel should come off easily now. Slice the tomato into 5 slices and set aside.

Use a biscuit cutter to cut the bread in circles the size of the tomato. Don't let the bread dry out at this point. Spread each circle with the mayonnaise, enough to be able to taste, but not so much as to squish out the sides of your mouth as you bite off a bit. Top with a tomato slice. Sprinkle with the salt and paprika, peppers, and the fresh herbs. These should, and will, be eaten within a couple of hours of preparation. Please avoid refrigeration. Cold temperatures turn a tomato's sugar into starch, hopelessly depriving the flavor factor.

Ingredients

2 tablespoons lemon juice
1 teaspoon salt
1 clove garlic, minced
1 teaspoon dry mustard
· Cayenne pepper to taste
   Black pepper to taste
2 egg yolks
1 pint vegetable oil

MAYONNAISE

MAKES ABOUT 1½ PINTS.

Preparation

Mix together the lemon juice, salt, garlic, mustard, and peppers in a mixing bowl. Place the yolks in the mixing bowl and start beating with an electric mixer. Pour in the oil in a thin, steady stream, beating constantly. The oil should "catch" and emulsify the mixture. The more oil you add, the thicker the mayonnaise. Add all of the oil and adjust the seasoning.

Mayonnaise will keep in the fridge for at least a week.

Ingredients

½ pound fresh goat cheese (or
   cream cheese)
1 teaspoon grated onion
   Large bunch watercress
   (about ¼ pound, cleaned,
   stemmed, and coarsely
   chopped)
   Zest and juice from ½
   lemon
   Freshly milled black pepper
   White or whole wheat bread

WATERCRESS SANDWICHES

Peppery watercress grows wild in the streams of Middle Tennessee. Just don't mind the creek snakes and don't pick more cress than you intend to eat in a day or so. It will go limp and puny overnight.

MAKES ENOUGH FOR ABOUT 2 DOZEN SANDWICHES.

Preparation

Mix together the goat or cream cheese, onion, watercress, lemon, and pepper. Let stand for 1 hour or so for the flavors to marry.

Spread the mixture thinly on the bread, which you may cut out however you choose. These sandwiches will keep well for a few hours.

COUNTRY HAM SANDWICHES

My great great grandmother, Kate Litton Cooper, recorded her version of this sandwich in her notebook, written in 1864.

MAKES ENOUGH FOR ABOUT 16 TEA-SIZED SANDWICHES.

Ingredients

- ¼ cup mustard
- ½ cup butter, softened
- 1 teaspoon black pepper
- Pinch sugar
- 1 tablespoon cider vinegar
- 8 slices homemade white bread
- ½ pound country ham, very thinly sliced
- 1 spring onion, sliced thin

Preparation

Mix together the mustard, butter, pepper, sugar, and vinegar. Spread onto the bread and lay the ham on half the slices. Top with the onion and the remaining dressed bread slices. Cut into thirds.

SAUSAGE PINWHEELS

MAKES ABOUT 2½ DOZEN.

Ingredients

- 1 recipe Buttermilk Biscuit dough (see recipe, page 160)
- ½ pound breakfast sausage

Preparation

Preheat the oven to 400°. Roll or pat out the dough in a rectangle ¼-inch thick. Thinly spread sausage over all. Roll up jelly roll style to a log no more than 2-inches in diameter. Slice into ½-inch pieces. This is much easier to do if you first chill the log. Place on a lightly greased cookie sheet and bake for 15 minutes, until the sausage is cooked and the dough is lightly browned. Serve warm.

Ingredients

- 1½ cups all-purpose flour
- 1 teaspoon baking powder
- ½ teaspoon salt
- ¼ teaspoon or more cayenne pepper
- ½ pound sharp Cheddar cheese, grated and brought to room temperature (see note)
- ¼ cup butter, softened

CHEESE STRAWS

I can't imagine life without cheese straws. Whenever I was living out of town and came home to visit, Mama knew that cheese straws were the one food item that she must have waiting. I would walk in the house, put down my bags, and proceed to the waiting tin on the kitchen counter. Having shoved several cheese straws into my mouth, I was then prepared to greet the patiently waiting members of my family. First things first.

There are several variations of this recipe, some with sesame or benne seeds or even Rice Krispies for crunch. My mother has always rolled the dough into a log, chilled the log, and then sliced off wafers to bake. You can keep an unbaked log in the fridge for unexpected guests for at least a week or so. I have to admit that I've always preferred the visuals of the true "straw" that is run through a cookie press or else hand sliced in strips and then cut into bite-size pieces. Whatever, I just crave the taste.

MAKES ABOUT 2 DOZEN.

Preparation

Preheat the oven to 350°. Mix together first 4 ingredients and stir in the cheese. Add the butter and mix well. Finish in one of three ways:

1. Roll the dough into a log, 1½ inches in diameter. Chill, and then slice off ⅓-inch thick wafers.

2. Or run the dough through the #1 disc of a cookie press into long strips, directly onto the ungreased cookie sheet.

3. Or roll out in a rectangle about ¼-inch thick. Use a knife to cut strips the length of the dough, then slice these strips into about 2-inch pieces.

Bake for 15 to 20 minutes. The thicker straws will take longer.

Slice the pressed straws into 2-inch pieces while they are still warm.

Delicious warm or at room temperature. Stored in an airtight tin, these will keep for a few days.

1   pound *sharp Cheddar cheese, grated*
¼   *onion, diced*
¼   *cup mayonnaise*
¼   *cup buttermilk*
1   *2-ounce can pimientos, diced, the juice reserved*
¼   *teaspoon cayenne pepper*

PIMIENTO CHEESE

I had always taken pimiento cheese for granted until I prepared some for a cross-cultural group of friends residing in the Virgin Islands. No one from anywhere in the world except the South had ever heard of pimiento cheese, and they all proclaimed me a genius for having created such a perfect food. Pimiento cheese is a very handy trick if you should find yourself in a spot with limited groceries.

The most traditional way to eat this is stuffed in the hollow of a celery stick. The contrast in textures and flavors is refreshing. It's also a nice filling for small tea sandwiches.

MAKES ABOUT 5 CUPS.

Preparation

Combine all in a bowl and mix well. Pimiento cheese will keep in the refrigerator for several days. Allow to come to room temperature before trying to spread.

GINGER DATE NUT BREAD WITH CREAM CHEESE

This is a dense, nutty bread, not too sweet, that we spread with a mixture of cream cheese and butter. It may sound simplistic, but it is simply heaven. I'll bet that these are a British tea-time import. My fondest memory of this sandwich is as a munchy that my sisters and I nibbled on in the back of our big old Buick on the eight-hour drive to Florida. We never stopped for our big picnic lunch until shortly after we spotted the first Spanish moss in the trees. Just south of Op, Alabama, land of opportunity, to be exact.

Preparation

Use the bread recipe found on page 167. Slice thin and then cut in circles. Spread generously with a mixture of equal amounts of cream cheese and butter, and top with another bread slice.

Ingredients

2 cups nasturtium flowers with
  several leaves
  Zest from 1 lemon
  Dash fresh squeezed lemon
  juice
18 thin slices whole wheat bread
1 cup fresh mild goat cheese
  (or cream cheese), softened

FLOWER SANDWICHES

When I really started exploring with cooking in the early eighties, I believed that edible flowers were just the epitome of moderne and sophisticated.

I have since found that every Southern cooking treatise I have read, from fifty to one hundred years old, uses nasturtiums, Johnny jump-ups, and borage in some very interesting ways. This idea is from my Aunt Kate Brew Vaughn. The peppery flowers are tasty with a mild cream or goat cheese.

MAKES ABOUT 36 SANDWICHES.

Preparation

Roughly chop the nasturtiums with the leaves and toss with the lemon juice and zest. Cut the bread in small shapes, circles or rectangles, getting 2 small sandwiches from each larger slice of bread. Spread the bread with the cheese and and top liberally with the nasturtium mix, lightly pressing it into the cheese. Cover loosely with a towel until ready to serve. Serve within 2 hours of assembling.

Ingredients

1 cup all-purpose flour
1/2 cup butter, softened
1/4 pound sharp Cheddar cheese,
  grated
2 tablespoons milk
1/4 cup marmalade or jelly

MARMALADE CHEESE PASTRIES

The cheese and marmalade are so good together. This dough cooks more like a cracker than the earlier cheese straws.

MAKES ABOUT 24 SMALL BISCUITS.

Preparation

Preheat the oven to 350°. Work together the flour, butter, and cheese. Mix in the milk to form a soft dough. Roll very thin on a floured surface and cut in small circles with the top of a spice jar. Use your finger to make an indentation and fill this with about 1/4 teaspoon of the marmalade. Place on a nonstick baking sheet and bake for about 15 minutes, until the bottoms are browned and the marmalade is bubbly.

OLIVES, DATES, OR ALMONDS IN CHEESE PASTRY

These used to be really popular, and I haven't seen them at a party in ages. They're delicious, too, and very pretty.

Preparation

P reheat the oven to 350°. Use the recipe for cheese dough from the Marmalade Cheese Pastries (recipe precedes) and roll ¼-inch thick. Cut out pieces large enough to encircle your chosen filling and wrap them completely in the dough. Place on a non stick baking sheet and bake for about 15 minutes, until golden brown.

Beaten Biscuits and Country Ham

I feel compelled to take a deep breath before I utter the words "Beaten Biscuits." As if I were ambassador to some obscure country of which someone has politely made query. I'd better make what I have to say brief yet interesting and informative. Most unfortunately, in my own sentiments, at least, most folks just aren't interested in hearing as much about beaten biscuits as I know. It was a hard blow, coming to the realization of the greater public's apathy concerning beaten biscuits. You see, they are sacred in my family; to my mind, a good deal holier than that wafer that dissolved in my mouth at church on the first Sunday of every month. The breaking of beaten biscuits occurred with much greater regularity. My family is Methodist when it comes to communion wafers and grape juice, but quite Catholic in regards to beaten biscuits and iced tea. Growing up, we knew that not everyone had a beaten biscuit resource, and we pitied those unfortunates. After all, making Beaten Biscuits was not only an all day affair, but it required special equipment and skilled training. My grandmother and my mother both owned hand driven beaten biscuit cranks. Similar to pasta machines, but much more cumbersome, these had to be bolted to the kitchen table and required two healthy participants, one to feed the stiff dough through the rollers, and the other to catch the dough on the other side and ease the dough on the remainder of its journey. This process was repeated again and again until the dough "blistered" in a gentle puffing pop, indicating that virtually all air had been forced out of the dough. Once formed, the biscuits themselves were cooked in a very slow oven and allowed to sit in that oven until the oven was completely cool. "Light and airy" are not the adjectives one would choose to describe a beaten biscuit. No more so than "quick and easy."

Beaten biscuits originated when leavening agents were not available. Their utterly dry and dense texture was developed into an attribute rather than a liability, as workers would take the biscuits with them in their pockets as they rode through and labored in the fields. Beaten biscuits do not get stale. Back at the house, beaten biscuits were daintily served on silver trays with their match made in culinary heaven, country ham. Long after the introduction of soda and yeast made a softer, more delicate pastry possible, beaten biscuits remained the party biscuit of choice.

The cultural impact of the beaten biscuit in Middle Tennessee is best illustrated in a story my grandmother, Anna Martha Cooper Frost, born in 1887, used to tell me about an overnight party she attended as a teenager. As a means of amusement there was a competition to see who could make the best beaten biscuits without the aid of a biscuit brake. I guess they didn't have Fuji boards or Twister to entertain themselves. The ingenious young woman who won, not my grandmother, used a baseball bat to beat the dough into submission.

I have heard vague theories that beaten biscuits may have originated in England. If that were so, I believe that their American realm would cover much more territory, given the prevailing British influence throughout all of the colonies. Since at least the beginning of this century, beaten biscuits seem to have been peculiarly exclusive to Middle Tennessee and Kentucky. Mother was slightly disappointed at the blank faces of even my Virginia college chums and their families upon the presentation of the noble biscuit on parents' day weekends. Even more disheartening was the thank you note received from some new summer camp friends from Texas who exclaimed of the tastiness of beaten biscuits with jelly. Oh, dear. Oh, no, not jelly. Beaten biscuits are to be eaten with butter, butter and country ham, or plain. Jelly simply doesn't do.

As long as my grandmother was in the beaten biscuit-making business, my mother stayed out of the spotlight. But as Grandmother, then in her late eighties, stepped aside for the next generation, mother shone in her role as the High Priestess of Beaten Biscuits.

Mother's beaten biscuits are requested at every affair of cultural or historical impact. Country fairs, annual club picnics, study groups, garden club and church picnics. And that's just in the summer. We have them at Thanksgiving, Christmas, New Year's Day, and Easter, as well as most family birthdays, graduations, Christenings, and funerals, and of course in honor of the homecomings of displaced relations who have unwittingly wandered away from the bosom of the Tennessee Valley. This keeps mother busy.

When Aunt Mary Linda died, mother inherited her motor powered beaten biscuit brake. This ingenious machine is your standard biscuit brake driven by the horsepower of a Singer sewing machine. In the 1920s many ladies had their brakes thusly converted. I know of only two in existence today.

Mother's beaten biscuit brake is set up in the play room, and Daddy is now her able assistant. I don't know that this has necessarily helped their relationship, but after forty-five years, you do what you have to for each other. After all, Daddy's got the best beaten biscuit connection going. I think he's rather proud of tending the brake now and then.

BEATEN BISCUITS

Ingredients

4   cups all-purpose flour
1   teaspoon salt
2   tablespoons cornstarch
1   to 2 tablespoons sugar
⅔   cup shortening (or lard)
1   cup half and half

There are a couple of variables here. Lard was originally used before we had vegetable shortening. Lard will give a richer, fuller flavor, but many people prefer the cleaner taste from shortening. Shortening is unquestionably healthier, but there are beaten biscuit purists who insist that only lard will make a true beaten biscuit. The second variable is the sugar. Mother changes the amount according to her mood. I lean toward the lesser.

You may use a food processor instead of a biscuit brake. My mother pooh-poohs the notion, but I think that you will be pleased with the results.

MAKES ABOUT 4 DOZEN.

Preparation

Sift the dry ingredients together, and work the fat in as you would for a pie crust. Mix in the half and half, and gather into a workable dough. Let rest in the fridge for about 30 minutes.

Preheat the oven to 300°. Run the dough through a biscuit brake several times, folding in half after each run, until the dough blisters. You should hear a little pop. If the dough cracks, pebbles, or is otherwise difficult before it blisters, let it rest for several minutes before continuing. Alternately, beat the dough with a rolling pin or baseball bat, or mix it in a strong food processor and let the dough run for a couple of minutes. The finished dough is very taut and smooth. Use a rolling pin to roll out about ½-inch thick. Cut in very small circles and prick each biscuit with the tines of a fork. Place on an ungreased baking sheet and bake for 30 minutes. Turn the oven down to 250° and bake for 30 more minutes. Turn the oven off and let the biscuits rest inside with the door closed until the oven is completely cold.

The biscuits split marvelously for spreading with sweet butter and filling with very thinly sliced country ham. As many times as I've had them, I salivate at the thought just like Pavlov's dog. Or is that Sarah's daughter?

6 eggs
1 tablespoon mayonnaise
1 teaspoon mustard
1 teaspoon pickle relish
   Dash cayenne pepper
12 small sprigs dill
   Paprika

STUFFED EGGS

No one in my family refers to deviled eggs, they are always simply stuffed. And a simple stuffing is usually the best. Mom used to try to sneak in a little curry powder, but Daddy would quickly call a halt to that nonsense.

MAKES 12 STUFFED EGG HALVES.

Preparation

Place the eggs in a pot and cover with water. Bring the water to a boil and cook for 10 minutes, boiling. Pour off the water and fill the pot with cold water. Let sit for 5 minutes. This makes the egg pull away from the shell, making them easier to peel.

Peel and rinse the eggs and cut in half lengthwise. Pop the cooked yolks into a mixing bowl and add the mayonnaise, mustard, relish, and pepper. Use a fork to mash the yolks, mixing them with the other ingredients. Taste for seasoning. Add a bit more mayonnaise if they seem too dry. If you make the mixture too wet, you can always cook some more eggs to add.

Use a teaspoon to refill the egg whites, mounding the filling up a bit. Garnish with a fresh dill sprig and a dash of paprika.

Chapter 3

SOUPS

One of my favorite chefs in culinary school has this to say about making soup, "If you think you are a chef because you can stick a piece of cow in the oven until it doesn't say moo, you got something to learn, my friend. Soup. That's where it shows if you know how to cook." While he is Italian and northern Italian at that, the art of soup making is a constant throughout the world. Soups have, should have at least, a subtlety that only happens through care, tasting, and a little intuition. Soups aren't as good if you just throw everything in the pot in no particular order and let her rip; and even when you follow a recipe ever so meticulously, you still have to stir and taste and make some decisions yourself. Whoever wrote that recipe is probably not in your kitchen looking at those vegetables, tasting that chicken stock, stirring those beans. I believe that in soup making a strength of devotion shines through, both to the soup and to whomever you're cooking it for. And I believe that kinder people make better soups.

Probably the most common Southern-style soup is a bean soup. Bean soups are practical. They're inexpensive, something you can make year round, and very filling—a point not to be overlooked if you have a big family or a few field hands to feed. No doubt these once all factored into the pervasive popularity of bean soups. But most of us today don't have to think too much about what foods are available at the market or what way to best fill several hungry tummies for as long as possible. These are, for the most part, affluent times, and bean soups the world around are essentially "peasant food." So there must be something more to this cheap and hearty fare, an essential ingredient not listed in many recipes, but definitely present in any pot of beans slow simmered in any kitchen. And that, my friends, is what I call soul satisfaction. That dreamy smile that wipes the frown lines away as you poke your head into the pot and lick your lips. The comforting sound your spoon makes scraping against the bottom of your bowl (especially when you know that there's more left in the pot). The warm glow inside your belly that spreads to all your toes and fingertips. That's the way a homemade bean soup should make you feel. And it feels even better to make one for someone you love.

I make bean soups with either fresh or dried beans. Obviously I use dried beans in the winter. I also tend to use dried beans for large batches of soup, as fresh beans are not so cheap as the dried variety. Frequently I use the traditionally Southern smoked pork seasoning when I make dried-bean soups. Smoked pork has been used as a seasoning in the South for centuries, lending a deep, distinctive flavor to so many dishes, particularly dried beans. The flavor of fresh beans themselves is so exquisite that I like to let the pure vegetable flavor shine through without any meat. Another variable in bean soup-making is whether or not to purée or strain the soup. I think that this is done more rarely these days, possibly being thought of as one more chore that could easily be cut out. While this is true, there's something so lovely about the velvety texture of smooth bean soup, and puréeing in a food processor will do the job almost as well as straining, and quite easily.

All that being said, I have included essentially three different methods for cooking bean soups. They may be varied by the other vegetables you use with the beans (bell peppers and carrots are two good options I didn't specify) and the type of beans you use. Beans all cook the same way, but they cook for different times, so beware. The idea of putting a pot of beans on the stove to cook all day without any attention is a myth. You must watch your beans and stir them now and then and occasionally add some liquid. Beans need attention just like everybody else. Enough already, here we go.

FRESH OCTOBER BEAN SOUP

A luscious soup that showcases the pure flavor of fresh beans.

ABOUT 1 GALLON.

2   quarts fresh October beans
      (or limas)
4   bay leaves
2   whole cloves plus 4 minced
      cloves garlic
3   teaspoons salt
1   gallon water
1   tablespoon olive oil
1   onion, chopped
¼   teaspoon black pepper
1   whole fresh cayenne pepper
2   fresh tomatoes, peeled and
      chopped
2   sprigs fresh thyme
4   sprigs parsley
½   bottle beer

Preparation

Rinse the beans and pick over. Place in a pot along with 2 of the bay leaves, 2 whole cloves of garlic, and 1 teaspoon of salt. Cover with water. Bring to a boil and cook the beans until just tender, about 15 to 20 minutes. Drain and rinse briefly.

Heat the olive oil in a soup pot and cook the onions over high heat, browning them partially, for about 5 minutes. Add the minced garlic and cook for a minute, then stir in the beans. Cover the beans with about 3 quarts of cold water and add the other 2 teaspoons of salt, the black pepper, and cayenne. Bring to a boil. Reduce the heat, maintaining a slow but steady boil. Cook the beans for about 15 minutes, then add the tomatoes, thyme, and parsley. Cook for 30 minutes, then add the beer. Stir well and cook another 15 minutes.

If the soup is too thick, you may thin it with water or beer. If the soup is still too runny, let it cook down a bit more. Some of the beans should have fallen apart, thickening the soup, while a few whole beans remain. Taste the soup for seasoning and adjust. Remove the bay leaves, thyme sprigs, and the stems from the parsley. Serve the soup hot.

Ingredients

1 quart black-eyed peas (white beans, kidneys, or pintos all work just as well)

1 pound pork trimmings (from country ham or hog jowl)

2 or 3 whole cayenne peppers, dried or fresh

2 bay leaves

3 quarts water

2 tablespoons olive oil

1 large onion, chopped

4 ribs celery, chopped

6 cloves garlic, minced

2 teaspoons dried thyme

2 teaspoons black pepper

DRIED BLACK-EYED PEA SOUP

A great snowy weekend soup. Any leftovers help you make it through the following week.

ABOUT 1 GALLON.

Preparation

Soak the beans in water overnight (this not only cuts down the cooking time, but also removes a lot of the material that causes gas).

The next morning, drain and rinse the beans. Place them in a large heavy pot along with the pork, cayenne peppers, and bay leaves, and cover with 3 quarts of cold water. Bring to a boil, stirring occasionally so that they don't scorch. Strain off the scum that rises to the top and turn down to simmer. Simmer until the beans are quite tender, and some have split open, thickening the soup.

While the beans are cooking, heat the oil in a skillet and sauté the onion, celery, and garlic with the thyme and pepper until the vegetables are translucent and slightly softened, about 10 minutes. Add these to the beans and cook about 30 minutes more. Remove the pork and skim the fat. Taste and adjust the seasoning, and serve with corn bread and hot sauce. Some people like to slice the pork thinly and serve the slivers on top of the soup bowl.

CREAMY WHITE BEAN SOUP

I like white beans to make a puréed soup because the skin of the bean is more tender to begin with and white beans have a rich flavor that lends itself well to a smooth soup.

Preparation

For a puréed bean soup, use the same quantities as for Black-eyed Pea Soup, simply substituting dried white beans for the dried black eyes. You might want to add 3 diced carrots to the vegetable mixture. They give the soup a little sweetness. Cook the vegetables in the olive oil, just as you do with the black eyes, then add the sautéed vegetables to the pot after 1 hour and cook them together with the white beans for 1 more hour. Remove the pork and either force the soup through a fine strainer or purée in a food processor.

Return the soup to the pot and cook for another 20 minutes, stirring frequently. Adjust the seasoning and serve.

Ingredients

2   teaspoons vegetable oil
1   onion, diced
1   quart chicken stock, heated
1   teaspoon salt
1/2 teaspoon black pepper
    Pinch cayenne pepper
6   medium yellow squash
    (actually, the smaller the
    better—if quite small, use
    8 or 10), scrubbed and
    sliced thin
2   cups buttermilk
1   tablespoon minced fresh dill
1   teaspoon minced fresh chives

COLD SQUASH AND BUTTERMILK SOUP

Consider this a summertime tonic. Refreshing, light, and zingy. A perfect lunch or early supper on the porch.

MAKES ABOUT 3 QUARTS.

Preparation

Heat the oil in a saucepan and add the onion. Cook for 5 minutes, then pour the stock into the saucepan and heat to a boil. Add the squash and cook for 15 minutes. Remove from the heat and let cool. Roughly purée the soup in the food processor, leaving some chunks. Pour into a bowl. Stir in the buttermilk and herbs. Let sit in the fridge for about 20 minutes, then taste and adjust seasoning. Serve cold.

COLD TOMATO SOUP WITH CUCUMBER AND MINT

Ingredients

- 4 ripe tomatoes, peeled, seeded, and finely chopped by hand or food processor
- ¼ red onion, finely chopped
- 2 cloves garlic, pushed through a press or very finely minced
- 3 scallions, thinly sliced
- 1 cucumber, quartered lengthwise and thinly sliced
- 2 tablespoons fresh mint, roughly chopped
- Juice of 2 lemons
- 1 cup tomato juice
- ½ cup chicken stock
- 2 teaspoons salt
- Pinch cayenne pepper
- ½ cup sour cream or yogurt to garnish

It would be very pretty to use a variety of some of the different heirloom tomatoes that come in shades of yellow, gold, orange, and burgundy. A few farmers' markets or specialty stores supply them, or they're very rewarding to grow yourself. Each tomato variety has its own unique flavor and texture, as well as color, adding dimensions of interest to your summer as well as your soup.

MAKES ABOUT 2 QUARTS.

Preparation

Peel the tomatoes by first coring them, then dropping into simmering water for 30 seconds. Remove from the hot water and place immediately in ice water. Slip the skin off and squeeze out most of the seeds. Chop finely and place in a bowl with all of the juice from the tomatoes. Add everything but the sour cream. Stir and let sit for 15 minutes. Taste and adjust the seasoning. Serve chilled with a dollop of sour cream.

3   quarts chicken stock
1   medium potato, peeled and thinly sliced
1   medium turnip, peeled and thinly sliced
1   parsnip, peeled and thinly sliced
2   carrots, peeled and thinly sliced
2   teaspoons salt
½   teaspoon white pepper
2   whole cayenne peppers
3   bay leaves
2   tablespoons olive oil
3   strong spring onions (or 1 yellow), peeled, quartered, and thinly sliced
6   cloves garlic, minced
¼   green cabbage, sliced thin then chopped in bite-sized pieces
    Juice of 1 lemon
4   scallions, thinly sliced
1   sprig fresh parsley minced

CABBAGE SOUP WITH ROOT VEGETABLES

This soup is so good and healthy. It's like a tonic to take the chill out your bones in the first promising days of spring.

MAKES ABOUT 1 GALLON.

Place the stock in a soup pot and bring to a boil. Add the potato, turnip, parsnip, and carrots along with the salt, pepper, cayenne, and bay leaves. Bring back to a hard boil and turn down to low.

Heat the olive oil in a large skillet and cook the onion over high heat for 5 minutes. Add the garlic and cabbage and cook on high, stirring, for 5 more minutes. Squeeze the juice from the lemon into the pan and remove from the heat. Place the contents of the skillet into the soup, stir, and let cook for 15 minutes. The root vegetables should be very tender and starting to break up. Retrieve the cayenne peppers from the soup, mince, and use as a garnish, if desired. Top with scallions and parsley. Sliced hard-boiled eggs and vinegar are also good ideas.

Ingredients

4   pounds beef for stew

1½ cups all-purpose flour,
      seasoned with 1 teaspoon
      salt and ½ teaspoon
      black pepper

5   tablespoons butter

1   cup red wine

1   gallon water

1   tablespoon salt

½   teaspoon black pepper

¼   teaspoon red pepper

2   bay leaves

2   onions, chopped

4   ribs celery, chopped

6   cloves garlic, minced

2   bell peppers, chopped

2   cups green beans, cut in 1-
      inch pieces

1½ cups corn kernels

1½ cups lima beans

3   medium potatoes, cut in 1-
      inch pieces

3   carrots, cut in 1-inch pieces

2   cups sliced okra

4   fresh tomatoes, peeled and
      chopped (or 1 large can)

2   cups chopped yellow squash

2   cups chopped zucchini

3   cups chopped cabbage

2   quarts beef stock

1   teaspoon oregano

1   teaspoon dried basil

2   tablespoons parsley

3   scallions, thinly sliced

VEGETABLE BEEF SOUP

Browning the beef gives the flavor more depth.

That long list of vegetables is just the tip of the iceberg for what you could employ. In the winter you can use frozen vegetables, and in the summer you can clean out the garden, your fridge, and the fridge of all of your neighbors, if you choose. Think about trying eggplant, cauliflower, turnips and parsnips, beans, pasta, barley or rice, etc. There are no "correct" quantities, just what feels good to you, which may mean whatever you have on hand or something in the market that inspires you. Be generous with the seasonings and the love. This will make or break your soup.

MAKES ABOUT 2 GALLONS.

Preparation

Rinse the beef and pat dry. Dredge in the flour. Heat 3 tablespoons of butter in a soup pot and brown the meat on all sides. If necessary, do this in batches to avoid overcrowding the pot. Pour in a little wine to help scrape up the browned bits on the bottom. Leave everything in the pot and cover with cold water. Add the salt, peppers, and bay leaves, and bring to a boil. Reduce the heat and simmer.

While the beef is cooking, heat the remaining butter in a skillet and sauté the onion, celery, and garlic for just about 10 minutes. Set aside. When the meat has cooked for 1 hour and 30 minutes, add the onion mixture along with the other ingredients, except the parsley and scallions. Bring everything to a boil and cook for another 30 minutes until the meat is very tender and the vegetables cooked through. Remove the bay leaf. The potatoes should start to break up a little and thicken the soup.

CHICKEN AND RICE SOUP

This is a wonderfully homey soup with terrific, rich flavor that can come only from making your own broth.

ABOUT 1 GALLON.

- 1 whole chicken
- 2 ribs celery
- 1 onion, quartered
- 3 bay leaves
- 1 teaspoon dry thyme
- 1 dried cayenne pepper
- 1/2 teaspoon black pepper

- 1 onion, chopped small
- 2 ribs celery, chopped small
- 2 carrots, peeled and chopped small
- 1 red bell pepper, ribbed and seeded, cut small
- 2 teaspoons fresh rosemary leaves, minced

- Juice of 2 lemons
- 2 cups cooked rice
- 1 tablespoon fresh chopped parsley
- 4 scallions, sliced thin

Preparation

Remove the giblets and discard or set aside for another use. Rinse the chicken well, inside and out. Place in a large pot with 2 ribs of celery, 1 onion, bay leaves, thyme, cayenne, and black pepper. Cover with water. Bring to a boil, skim any scum that rises, stir, and reduce the heat to a simmer. Simmer the chicken uncovered for 40 minutes. Remove the chicken and let cool. Strain the broth, skim off as much fat as possible, and continue to simmer while you prepare the remaining ingredients.

Add the chopped onion, celery, carrots, bell pepper, and rosemary to the broth and cook for 40 minutes, until the vegetables are tender. Meanwhile, pull off the chicken meat and tear into slightly larger than bite-size pieces. When the vegetables are tender, add the chicken to the broth along with the lemon juice and the rice. Simmer for 5 minutes. Stir in the parsley and scallions and serve hot.

¼ cup olive oil

1 large onion, chopped

4 cloves garlic, minced

1 green bell pepper, ribbed,
    seeded, and chopped

1 red or yellow bell pepper,
    ribbed, seeded, and
    chopped

2 cups limas, rinsed

3 large tomatoes, peeled and
    chopped

2 teaspoons salt

½ teaspoon black pepper

¼ teaspoon cayenne pepper
    Kernels from 6 ears corn

2 tablespoons chopped fresh
    basil

1 tablespoon chopped fresh
    parsley

3 scallions, sliced thin

1½ teaspoons red wine vinegar
    Juice of 1 lemon

SUCCOTASH

Succotash was originally a native American vegetable stew made largely of corn. Today there are many varieties. Succotash can be a hearty and comforting winter time meal made convenient and delicious with frozen corn, or it can be a celebration of summer itself when the corn is high, the limas are fresh, and the tomatoes are ripe. This is my summertime version. It can be adapted to any January day by merely visiting your freezer section and probably adjusting the seasoning.

MAKES ABOUT 1 GALLON, AT LEAST 12 SERVINGS.

Preparation

Heat the olive oil in a heavy pot or kettle and sauté the onions on high heat, browning them a little, for about 5 minutes. Add the garlic and peppers and cook for 5 more minutes. Stir in the limas and add water to cover, along with ½ teaspoon of salt. Bring to a boil and cook until the limas are just tender, about 10 to 15 minutes. Add the tomatoes with all of their juice, and the rest of the salt and peppers. Cook for 10 minutes, then add the corn. Cook another 10 minutes, then add the basil, parsley, scallions, vinegar, and lemon juice. Taste and adjust the seasonings. Serve as a stew over rice.

Chapter 4

SALADS

Salads allow your creativity to fly. It's hard to tie a person down to a real recipe for a salad because so much depends on what kind of mustard happens to be in your refrigerator that day, what type of vinegar is open, how many bell peppers you have. These may account for subtle distinctions, but subtlety is what good food is all about. Changing a recipe doesn't necessarily make it worse or better; it does make it yours. All of these salads are things I have made countless times, probably never exactly the same way twice. I always encourage spontaneity, especially with salads!

3 pounds potatoes, red or yellow thin-skinned variety,
   local if possible
½ yellow onion, finely diced
½ green bell pepper, diced
½ red bell pepper, diced
4 ribs celery, diced
4 scallions, cut thin
1 bunch parsley, minced
1 cup homemade mayonnaise
   (or Hellman's)
½ cup mustard
1 teaspoon salt
½ teaspoon white pepper
½ teaspoon black pepper
¼ teaspoon cayenne pepper
¼ cup paprika

POTATO SALAD

*I resoundingly believe that potato salad is best served while still a lit-
tle warm. I love hot sauce on potato salad, or if I'm lucky enough to
be at a barbecue, a bit of the barbecue sauce. I also know people who
eat potato salad between slices of white bread, as a sandwich with
catsup, and I know a couple of Cajuns who like to sink a spoonful of
potato salad in their gumbo.*

SERVES ABOUT 12.

Preparation

Scrub the potatoes, and cut into large pieces. Just cover with
well salted water and bring to a boil. Boil about 10 to 15 minutes,
until cooked through, but slightly firm to the fork. Drain, but do
not rinse. Let cool. Combine the potatoes with the other ingredients in a large bowl. Stir to mix and adjust the seasoning.

The more you stir, the more your potatoes will mash. That's
why I like to keep the potato pieces pretty large. They're just
about salad size by the time you're finished mixing.

8 hard-boiled eggs, peeled and
   chopped
¼ red onion, diced
2 tablespoons mayonnaise
2 tablespoons mustard
½ teaspoon fresh parsley or
   mint

EGG SALAD

Makes a great sandwich with cucumber.

SERVES 4 TO 6.

Preparation

Mix all together in a bowl. If the mixture is too runny, just boil
some more eggs, chop them, and add to the salad.

- ½ head red cabbage, very thinly sliced
- ½ head white cabbage, very thinly sliced
- ½ yellow onion, very thinly sliced
- 2 carrots, grated
- 3 scallions, thinly sliced
- ½ cup white vinegar
- ⅔ cup mayonnaise
- ⅓ cup yellow mustard
  Juice of 1 lemon
- ¼ teaspoon white pepper
  Few squirts hot sauce
- ½ teaspoon salt

COLE SLAW

Here in Tennessee, we like to put cole slaw on barbecued sandwiches. A must-have for a fish fry, too.

SERVES ABOUT 8.

Preparation

Mix everything together and adjust the seasoning and consistency to suit your taste.

This recipe is kind of a mongrel. There are a million ways to make cole slaw. I took what I like best about several cole slaws and threw them all together.

Ingredients

- 4 home-grown tomatoes, cored and cut into 8 wedges
- 2 cucumbers, peeled in strips and cut in ½-inch circles
- ½ red onion, very thinly sliced
  Juice of 1 lemon
- 2 tablespoons red wine vinegar
- 4 tablespoons olive oil
- ¼ cup mint leaves, cut in thin strips
- ½ teaspoon salt
  Several grinds black pepper

TOMATO AND CUCUMBER SALAD

A classic summer salad. So refreshing.

SERVES 8.

Preparation

Toss it all together in a salad bowl and taste for seasoning. There's lots of room for experimenting with this recipe.

TOMATO ASPIC

It took me years to find a tomato aspic I could proudly serve. This one is based on my grandmother's. It's very snappy and tasty, too.

SERVES 6 TO 8.

Ingredients

- 1 package unflavored gelatin
- 1/4 cup cold water
- 1 16-ounce can tomatoes
- 1 onion, sliced
- 3 ribs celery
- 1 teaspoon salt
- 1 tablespoon Worcestershire sauce
- Juice and zest of 3 lemons
- 1/4 teaspoon cayenne pepper
- 1/4 teaspoon black pepper
- 1 tablespoon chopped fresh basil
- 1 tablespoon chopped fresh parsley
- 2 teaspoons snipped chives

Preparation

Soak the gelatin in cold water. Simmer together the rest of the ingredients except the fresh herbs until the tomatoes are thoroughly softened. Push through a sieve over the gelatin. Stir in the fresh herbs and pour into a greased mold. Let set up in the refrigerator.

You may set pieces of cucumber and celery or whole shrimp in the aspic. Push the garnish all the way to the bottom of the mold so that you can see it when it is unmolded. To unmold, wet a dishcloth with very hot water. Run this along the mold to loosen it. Place a platter over the mold and invert. If the aspic doesn't fall right out, continue rubbing a wet, hot towel over the mold.

3 **pounds fresh baby limas, shelled and rinsed**

   Water to cover

4 **cloves garlic**

2 **teaspoons salt**

1 **teaspoon cayenne pepper**

1/4 **cup best olive oil**

   Juice and zest of 2 lemons

1/4 **cup fresh parsley, roughly chopped**

1/2 **bunch green onions, sliced thin**

LIMA BEAN SALAD

This is a salad for July, for those few precious weeks when the fresh baby limas are out. When the good Lord provides a vegetable this sublime, you don't want to insult Him by messing with it too much.

SERVES 8 TO 10.

Preparation

Place the limas in a pot and cover with cold water. Add the garlic, salt and cayenne and bring to a boil. Skim off the scum that rises to the top, stir, and turn the heat to medium. Cook uncovered until the limas are cooked through and tender, about 15 minutes. Drain the limas, discarding the garlic cloves and bay leaf. Place the limas in a bowl and pour the olive oil over them while the beans are still warm. Zest the lemons and squeeze the lemon juice into the bowl, avoiding any seeds. When the beans have cooled to room temperature, stir in the zest, fresh herbs, and cracked black pepper to taste. Check for salt and serve the beans at room temperature. These can keep for several hours in the refrigerator, but be sure to bring them fully back to room temperature or the flavor will be greatly sacrificed.

Ingredients

3   pounds fresh black-eyed
      peas (or 1 pound dried)
1   gallon water
    Salt to taste
1   teaspoon white pepper
1   teaspoon black pepper
2   bay leaves
3   cloves garlic
    Juice of 2 lemons
2   tablespoons red wine
      vinegar
2   teaspoons dried mustard
1/2 teaspoon salt
1/2 teaspoon black pepper
1   cup olive oil
1   sweet onion (Vidalia), diced
3   stalks celery, diced
1   red bell pepper, diced
2   home-grown tomatoes,
      chopped
1/2 cup chopped fresh basil
2   scallions, thinly sliced

BLACK-EYED PEA SALAD

SERVES 8.

Preparation

If using dried beans, sort and rinse and soak overnight in water. Drain and rinse before proceeding. If using fresh beans, rinse and sort.

Bring water to boil with salt, peppers, bay leaves, and garlic cloves. Add the beans and return to a boil. Skim any scum that comes to the surface. Reduce the heat to medium and cook until the beans are cooked through but not mushy, about 1 hour and 30 minutes for the dried and 20 minutes for the fresh.

While the beans are cooking, mix together the lemon juice, vinegar, mustard, salt, black pepper, and olive oil as for a salad dressing.

When the beans are cooked, drain but do not rinse. Set in a large mixing bowl and pour the dressing over. Let sit until cool. Combine with the remaining ingredients and adjust the seasoning. The salad should sit for at least 30 minutes to allow the flavors to blend.

FRESH THREE BEAN SALAD

1 pound fresh shelled October
beans

3 cloves garlic, peeled

2 bay leaves

2 teaspoons salt

1 pound fresh snap beans

1 pound fresh wax beans

1 tablespoon salt

1 onion, sliced in thin
circles

3 stalks celery, thinly sliced
on the bias

3 mild banana peppers, sliced
in thin rings

$\frac{1}{2}$ cup olive oil

$\frac{1}{3}$ cup red wine vinegar

$\frac{1}{4}$ cup sugar

Black pepper to taste

I have a strong hunch that before there were three cans of beans in the three bean salad, fresh October beans stood in the stead of pintos. Octobers are actually in season in July, right along with string and wax beans. This salad is an American classic which we need to rescue from the lame salad bars across the country. Let's get it out from behind that spit bar and back in the sunshine in the middle of the picnic table, proudly shouldering up to the potato salad and cole slaw.

SERVES ABOUT 12.

Preparation

Rinse the October beans and place in a pot. Cover by 4 inches with cold water and add the garlic cloves, bay leaves, and salt. Bring to a boil, skim the scum that rises, stir, and turn the heat down a bit. Continue to cook about 20 to 30 minutes until tender but not mushy. Drain and rinse under cold water, reserving the garlic cloves.

String the snap and wax beans. Bring a large pot of water with the tablespoon of salt to a rolling boil. Drop in the beans together and cook about four minutes, until crisp-tender. Drain and run under cold water until the beans are cool, to stop the cooking.

Place the three varieties of beans together in a large mixing bowl. Add the onion, celery, and peppers.

Mince the reserved garlic cloves and mix in a bowl with the olive oil. Pour the vinegar over the sugar and stir to dissolve. Whisk the vinegar and sugar into the olive oil. Pour the dressing over the vegetables. Taste, and add salt and black pepper to taste. Let the salad marinate for at 30 minutes before serving. Will last for 3 days in the refrigerator.

1 pound fresh beets

1 pound new potatoes

2 small spring onions, cut in
   thin circles

6 eggs

1 large bunch watercress

1½ cups True French Dressing
   (recipe follows)

BEET AND NEW POTATO SALAD

Many of the "composed" salads from our Southern heritage are a bit long on the mayonnaise and sugar for most contemporary tastes — mine at least. That said, I was delighted to discover some suggestions from the last century for really exciting combinations for cold salads. One of my favorites is a lusty and satisfying marriage of beets, new potatoes, and hard-boiled eggs. This is a visual feast, as well.

SERVES 6 TO 8.

Preparation

Trim the beets and boil in salted water about 15 minutes until tender. Cooking time will vary with their size and freshness. When they are easily pierced with a fork, drain and let cool. When they are cool enough to handle, peel (the skins slip off fairly easily) and slice in halves or quarters, depending on their size. Don't worry, the pink on your hands will eventually wash away.

Scrub the potatoes clean and cut in halves or quarters, depending on their size. Boil in salted water until tender but not mushy, about 10 to 15 minutes. Drain and set aside.

Place the eggs in a pot and cover with water. Bring to a boil and cook for ten minutes, boiling. Drain off the water, leaving the eggs in the pot. Refill with cold water. Set aside.

Pick through and rinse the watercress.

Place the potatoes, onions, and beets in a large mixing bowl and pour the dressing over. Toss the salad, watching the onions and potatoes turn intriguing shades of pink. Let the salad marinate in the dressing for at least 30 minutes.

Peel the eggs and cut lengthwise into quarters. Lay the watercress on a platter and mound the salad on top. Garnish with the egg wedges and grind some black pepper on top.

TRUE FRENCH DRESSING

Ingredients

1/4 cup vinegar (white or red wine)
  Juice of 1 lemon
1 tablespoon grated onion
1 clove garlic, well minced (optional)
1 teaspoon minced fresh parsley
1 teaspoon paprika
1 teaspoon dry mustard
1 teaspoon salt
1 cup olive oil

Most Southerners, with the exception of the Cajuns and Creoles, have not traditionally used a lot of garlic. Raw garlic, and in some cases raw onion, was considered, well, impolite. Recipes that did use garlic would frequently call for merely rubbing the salad bowl with the crushed clove. That doesn't quite get it for me. I say chop it up and toss it in. Life's just too short.

MAKES ABOUT 1½ CUPS.

Preparation

Mix the vinegar with the spices and beat in the olive oil. Let sit for 30 minutes before using.

PICKLED BEET SALAD

Ingredients

2 pounds fresh beets
2 small white onions, very thinly sliced
3/4 cup white vinegar
  Pinch salt
  Pinch cayenne pepper

Keep some in the fridge to perk up any meal in a hurry.

SERVES 6 TO 8.

Preparation

To cook fresh beets, which have much more flavor than canned ones, first rinse the beets well. Then trim both ends of the beets and boil in salted water for about 25 minutes, until fork tender. Drain and cool, then rub the skin away. Slice the beets in ½-inch circles. Toss with the remaining ingredients and let stand at least 1 hour to let the beets marinate.

MARINATED BRUSSELS SPROUTS

Ingredients

- 2 pounds fresh Brussels sprouts
- 3 quarts water
- 2 teaspoons salt
- 1 tablespoon capers, chopped
- 2 scallions, thinly sliced

- 2 cloves garlic, minced
- 3 tablespoons red wine vinegar
- 1 teaspoon dry mustard
- 1/2 teaspoon crushed black pepper
- Additional salt, as needed
- Juice and zest of 1 lemon
- 1/2 cup olive oil

I know that I emote a lot about a lot of vegetables, but I really, really love Brussels sprouts. Imagine, little mini cabbages growing on a bush! To put a whole Brussels sprout in your mouth and bite through all of that pungent flavor and goodness. How did God come up with this stuff? This salad helps get me through the winter blues. I found one very similar in some family writings from the turn of the century.

SERVES 6.

Preparation

Clean and trim the Brussels sprouts and cut in half, lengthwise. Bring the water to a boil with the salt and add the Brussels sprouts. Bring to a boil and cook until tender, about 5 minutes. Drain the sprouts and run under cold water. Place in a bowl with the capers and scallions.

In a separate bowl whisk together the remaining ingredients except the oil. Pour the oil into the rest, whisking until emulsified. Pour the dressing over the salad. Taste and adjust seasoning. Let the salad sit for at least 30 minutes to allow the flavors to marry. Serve at room temperature.

Ingredients

2   apples, fresh tart locals or
    Granny Smith
1   stalk celery, thinly sliced
    Juice of ½ lemon
½   bag spinach, cleaned and
    trimmed
½   cup black walnut pieces
    (English walnuts may be
    used)
4   scallions, thinly sliced
½   cup Blue Cheese Dressing
    (recipe follows)

APPLE AND WALNUT SALAD WITH BLUE CHEESE DRESSING

This a beautiful autumn salad. Perfect for a luncheon or for a light supper.

SERVES 4.

Preparation

Rinse the apples and slice in thin wedges, leaving the peel intact. Toss with the celery and lemon and set aside.

Preheat the oven to 400°. Place the nuts on a baking sheet and roast for about 5 minutes. Careful, they burn really easily.

Divide the spinach between 4 salad plates and casually arrange the apples on top. Sprinkle nuts and scallions over and drizzle with Blue Cheese Dressing.

Ingredients

6   tablespoons blue cheese
½   cup olive oil
1   clove garlic, minced
¼   teaspoon white pepper
¼   teaspoon paprika
½   teaspoon salt
3   tablespoons vinegar

BLUE CHEESE DRESSING

This old-fashioned blue cheese dressing has a devoted following. This is a classic for a reason: it's just so darned tasty.

MAKES A LITTLE OVER 1 CUP.

Preparation

Crumble the cheese and mix into the oil. Mix the garlic and seasonings into the vinegar. Pour the oil into the vinegar, stirring well.

Ingredients

½	cup sugar
⅓	cup red wine vinegar
1	teaspoon dry mustard
1	teaspoon salt
1	teaspoon paprika
1	cup vegetable oil
2	tablespoons poppy seeds

POPPY SEED DRESSING FOR FRUIT SALAD

Fruit salad should be as seasonal as the farmers' market. Apples, pears, and citrus are natural in cold weather months, while melons and berries shine in the summer. This traditional dressing shines through all the seasonings.

MAKES ABOUT 1 PINT, ENOUGH FOR 12 TO 16 SERVINGS OF FRUIT.

Preparation

Mix the sugar with the vinegar to dissolve. Stir in the mustard, salt, and paprika. Whisk in the oil and stir in the seeds. Whisk together briskly before serving.

CHICKEN SALAD

Ingredients

- 8 chicken breasts, bone in and skin on (this will give more flavor, but in a big hurry, use boneless-skinless and cut down the cooking time)
- ½ teaspoon salt
- ¼ teaspoon white pepper
- ¼ teaspoon black pepper
  Pinch cayenne pepper
- 1 teaspoon fresh thyme leaves (or ½ teaspoon dried)
- 2 cloves fresh garlic, thinly sliced
- 3 stalks celery, finely chopped
- ¼ red onion, finely chopped
- ¼ cup mayonnaise
- ⅓ cup buttermilk
- 1 tablespoon dijon mustard
- 1 tablespoon chopped fresh parsley

To this day, every day, I am newly astonished at just how much chicken salad people that live around here can and will eat. It boggles the mind. Needless to say, the "correct" chicken salad is a topic of heated dispute. For example, my mother uses a boiled dressing, which she will swear to you is the only honorable way to dress chicken salad. Sorry Mom, I like mine better, and it's much easier, too.

Although I am a thigh-eater at heart, I use only white meat for traditional Southern chicken salad. I like the milder flavor with the other simple ingredients.

This is a very basic chicken salad recipe. It can be gussied up for a fancier occasion with toasted sliced almonds or walnut halves and halved grapes. This version is nice in a lettuce cup with some finger sandwiches for a luncheon.

In our neck of the woods, you will find chicken salad between slices of bread, in a tomato, in an avocado half, in a hollowed out pineapple wedge and stuffed in pastry puffs, and almost always inside almost every refrigerator.

SERVES ABOUT 12 TO 16.

Preparation

Rub the chicken breasts with the salt, peppers, and thyme, getting up under the skin, and push the garlic slices under the skin as well. Pull the skin back over the flesh and roast the breasts at 400° for 20 or so minutes, until cooked through and the juices run clear. Do not overcook.

When cool enough to handle, remove the skin and discard. Discard the garlic slices. Pull the meat from the bone, tearing into larger than bite-sized pieces, not too small. Mix with the remaining ingredients.

Ingredients

- 3   pounds shrimp
- 1   gallon water
- 2   lemons
- 2   green onions, roughly chopped
- 3   sprigs parsley
- 1   celery stalk, chopped
- 1   bay leaf
- 2   teaspoons black pepper
- 1   teaspoon cayenne pepper

- 1/2   cup good olive oil
- 1   tablespoon white wine vinegar
- 4   lemons, juiced and zested
- 3   cloves garlic
- 1/4 to 1/2 teaspoon black pepper
- 1   ounce fresh parsley leaves
- 1/2   ounce fresh dill
  Salt to taste
- 1/2   red onion, finely chopped
- 3   stalks celery, diced
- 1   red bell pepper, diced
- 1   banana pepper (or hot pepper), seeded and finely chopped
- 1 1/2   tablespoons capers, roughly chopped

MARINATED SHRIMP SALAD

I love this salad in the heat of the summer. No matter how wilted people may feel, they can always eat shrimp. They can eat quite a lot of shrimp, as a matter of fact. I always make more than I think I could possibly need, and I never have leftovers.

SERVES ABOUT 6 AS A MAIN COURSE.

Preparation

Rinse the shrimp. Bring the water to a rolling boil with 2 lemons, green onions, parsley sprigs, 1 celery stalk, bay leaf, and black and cayenne pepper. Throw in the shrimp and bring back to a boil. Cook for about 4 minutes. You can tell that the shrimp are done when the meat pulls slightly away from the shell. Don't overcook!

When the shrimp are cooked, pull the pot from the heat and throw ice into the water to stop the cooking. This way the shrimp are still soaking up the flavors of the liquid without overcooking. If the ice melts very quickly add some more. You can drain and peel the shrimp in about 5 minutes.

Place the olive oil, vinegar, lemon juice, lemon zest, garlic, black pepper, parsley, dill, and salt to taste in the blender and purée until combined and smooth. Cut the shrimp in a little larger than bite-size pieces and place in a glass or ceramic bowl along with the remaining salad ingredients. Pour the dressing over and toss. The amount of salt you will need for the dressing depends on the saltiness of the shrimp. Some shrimp will be very salty when you purchase it, others not. You'll have to taste for yourself.

This salad is so refreshing, it's perfect for summer, served with avocados or tomatoes, or simply on a bed of lettuce. The flavor will improve for several hours after marinating, but it should be eaten by the following day.

Chapter 5

VEGETABLES AND SIDES

A Southern table is made heavy by the vegetable dishes and side items. Meat may be scarce, but greens, cornmeal, and potatoes rarely are. For centuries Southern cooks have used their ingenuity and imagination to concoct a startlingly vast and varied array of offerings made from what nature, a little farming, and a little milling provided. A traditional Southern dinner would probably have five or so side dishes, plus some sliced tomatoes and onions and a pickle tray. I have gone through the alphabet, filing my vegetables and sides accordingly. I could go back through and write about twice as many. But then what would I write about next time? These should provide a little inspiration. Starting with "A:"

Ingredients

2 bunches asparagus
1 gallon water
1 tablespoon salt
1 gallon ice water
2 teaspoons butter
1 teaspoon fresh dill

SIMPLE ASPARAGUS

Asparagus is wildly popular with my friends, family, and clients. I don't believe that we have quite adapted to the year round availability of the vegetable and, unlike many grocery store staple vegetables, which are too often woody and bland, we still rightly value asparagus as a precious object. Even though I can find it in my grocery store any time, I most treasure the taste of asparagus in the spring, when the earth is fresh and green and the first sprouts and bittersweet vegetables are bursting into our lives. Everyone cooked their asparagus a good deal longer twenty, even ten years ago. But now, all the folks I encounter, with the exception of my father, prefer their asparagus lightly cooked.

SERVES 6.

Preparation

Snap the asparagus stalks off just above the woody ends and discard ends. Bring the water to boil with the salt. Drop the asparagus in and let cook for 1 or 2 minutes after the water has regained its boil. Strain off the asparagus and toss it with the butter and dill. Serve immediately.

If you wish to hold the asparagus before serving, plunge it into ice water after it is drained. To serve, strain from ice water and reheat in a pan with melted butter until warm through. Toss with dill and serve.

MARINATED ASPARAGUS

This is a marvelous picnic or party item. I strongly urge considering asparagus a finger food. Its much more fun that way. The longer the asparagus sits in the marinade, the less vibrant its green color. As a trade off, the yummy taste of the marinade becomes more pronounced.

SERVES 6.

Ingredients

1   gallon salted water
2   bunches asparagus
1   gallon ice water

⅔ cup olive oil
¼ cup white wine vinegar
    Juice of 1 lemon
½ teaspoon salt
½ teaspoon cracked black
    pepper
1   clove garlic, minced
1   teaspoon chopped fresh dill
1   teaspoon chopped fresh mint
1   teaspoon chopped fresh
    parsley

Preparation

Bring the salted water to a boil (salt not only flavors the asparagus, it enhances the bright green color). Add the asparagus and cook for just 1 to 2 minutes. Drain and plunge the asparagus into ice water to stop the cooking.

Mix together the remaining marinade ingredients and pour over the drained asparagus in a noncorrosive container. Allow the asparagus to sit in the marinade for at least 30 minutes and up to 2 hours, depending on how concentrated you care for the flavor to be. If you refrigerate, allow to come to room temperature before serving.

Ingredients

1   gallon salted water

2   bunches asparagus

1   tablespoon chervil or parsley

⅔ cup cream

½ cup fresh goat cheese, or
    grated cheese of your
    choice

1   tablespoon minced chives
    Salt and black pepper

ASPARAGUS GRATIN

YES! Fresh farm cheese, cow and goat, was common in the South and most of the nation before the depression and the general move away from individual farms and towards large corporate dairies. Most farm wives made their own simple, tart cheese with the curds left over after milking.

In the last few years the face of cheese making has changed dramatically in this country. Once again there are small dairies scattered across the country, free-grazing their own herds of cattle, goats, or sheep, and producing everything from organic milk and butter to fresh, hand-ladled cheeses and more complex cooked and aged cheeses—a huge variety. In some communities local cheeses are found at the farmers' markets, while many gourmet grocers seek out these artisan cheeses. Seek out a few yourself. Smell and taste, and celebrate the notion of thinking small and taking a few steps backwards now and then!

SERVES 6.

Preparation

Snap off the asparagus just above the woody ends. Bring the salted water to a boil and cook the asparagus for 2 minutes. Drain. Lay the asparagus in a casserole. Stir the chervil into the cream and pour the cream over the asparagus. Dot with goat cheese and sprinkle the chives over. Bake at 400° for 10 to 15 minutes, until the cream is thickened. If the cheese is not browned, turn your oven setting to broil and brown the top of the gratin for about 5 minutes. Serve at once.

Chervil is a delicate spring herb I like to use, especially in the spring. Mint, dill, or parsley would all be good substitutes if you can't find the chervil.

Ingredients

- 1   28-ounce can pintos, drained
- 1   28-ounce can white kidneys, drained
- 6   slices bacon
- 1   yellow onion, diced
- 1   green bell pepper, diced
- 1   red bell pepper, diced
- 5   cloves garlic (or more), minced
- 3   tablespoons tomato paste
- 1/4   cup yellow mustard
- 1/4   cup molasses
- 1/4   cup firmly packed dark brown sugar
- 1   tablespoon vinegar cayenne hot sauce (such as Crystal)
- 2   teaspoons cider vinegar
- 1   teaspoon Worcestershire sauce
- 1/2   teaspoon salt
- 1/2   teaspoon black pepper

BAKED BEANS

While a smoking grill can make your patio smell like the Fourth of July, baked beans will do the same for your kitchen. These are a little sweet, a little tangy, rich and flavorful. Don't save them for just one day.

SERVES 12.

Preparation

Drain and rinse the beans well. Combine the beans in a large mixing bowl and set aside.

Cook the bacon in a skillet until crispy. Pull out the bacon and drop in the onions. Cook in the bacon drippings until translucent, then add the peppers and the garlic. Cook just to wilt the vegetables, 5 or so minutes. Add the vegetables to the beans, along with remaining ingredients except the bacon. Mix, taste, and adjust to suit you. Pour into a casserole, cover, and bake at 350° for 40 minutes. Remove the cover and crumble the bacon on top. Put back in the oven, uncovered, for 10 more minutes.

3 pounds fresh green or pole
beans, stringed
1/3 pound country ham or fat
back
1 yellow onion, sliced
2 pods dried cayenne pepper
2 teaspoons salt
6 new potatoes, quartered
Vinegar

COUNTRY-STYLE GREEN BEANS

SERVES 8.

Preparation

Place the beans, ham or fat back, and onion in a stock pot, along with the cayenne and salt. Cover with cold water and bring to a boil. Turn to low heat and cook until the beans are very tender, 1 hour or so. Add the potato quarters and cook until tender, another 20 minutes. If you like, remove the ham, cut or tear into small pieces, and put back in the pot.

The "pot licker" from this dish is so good, you may like to serve the beans in a bowl, along with corn bread to mop up that tasty juice.

Ingredients

2 pounds green beans, stringed
and cleaned
1 gallon water
1 tablespoon salt
3 tablespoons homemade Chili
Sauce (see recipe, page 4)

GREEN BEANS WITH CHILI SAUCE

This was the "city" way to serve green beans in my home.

SERVES 6.

Preparation

Bring water and salt to a boil. Add green beans and cook 5 to 10 minutes until tender.

Strain, toss with chili sauce, and serve immediately.

This is good the next day served cold.

SUMMER GREEN BEANS WITH HERBS

You can really only make this with very fresh tender beans. So many beans grow tough and stringy. My test is to eat a few raw. If they're good like that, they'll be great like this.

SERVES 6.

Ingredients

2½   pounds green beans
1   gallon water
1   tablespoon salt
1   tablespoon butter
½   teaspoon white pepper
4   leaves sorrel, cut in strips
4   leaves mint, cut in strips
1   tablespoon minced chives
    Juice of 1 lemon

Preparation

Rinse the beans and string, if necessary. Trim off the stem end, and the tip end, if desired. Prepare a large bowl of ice water. Bring 1 gallon of water to a boil with the salt and drop in the beans. Cook uncovered to desired state of doneness (I cook mine about 3 minutes). Drain the beans and plunge into ice water to stop the cooking and preserve the color.

Melt the butter in the same pan. Drain the beans again and add to the pan, along with the minced herbs, lemon juice, pepper, and additional salt, if necessary. Toss the beans in the pan to coat evenly with the herb butter. Heat through and serve.

Ingredients

2 pounds baby limas or butter beans

4 to 5 cups water, to cover the beans generously

1 teaspoon salt

¼ cup butter

BUTTER BEANS

You'll have to ask him yourself, but I believe that this is my father's favorite vegetable ever. He buys bushels of them in the summer, shucks them himself, and freezes them, so he can have good butter beans all winter. Last June he still had some left from the summer before that hadn't been used up during the winter. Still, his eyes shone brightly when he told me that the fresh beans would be ready the following week, like a child at Christmas.

This is how Daddy cooks butter beans.

SERVES 4 TO 6.

Preparation

Rinse the beans well. Bring the water to boil with the salt and butter. Add the beans and bring back to a boil. Reduce heat to medium and cook the beans for about 30 minutes. Serve hot.

OCTOBER BEANS

Ingredients

2 pounds October beans
1 thick slice fat back or slab bacon, or a little trimming from country ham
1/2 onion, chopped
1 cayenne pepper, dried or fresh, left whole

October beans are available along with the other fresh peas during those precious weeks of July. You wish you could spread out the bounty a little. I just find myself cooking peas and beans every day for several weeks. No one at home has complained yet.

Octobers get nice and soupy when you cook them down with a little pork. Perfect with corn bread. Look in the soups and salads sections for other ideas for October beans.

SERVES 8.

Preparation

Rinse the beans and set aside. Place the pork in a large pot with about 2 quarts of water. Bring to a boil and stir in the beans and onion and the pepper. Add more water if needed to cover the beans by at least 3 inches. Bring back to a boil, skim any scum that comes to the top, and turn the beans down to medium. Cook the beans about 20 minutes until tender. Taste the beans and season with salt, if needed. Remember, the pork is very salty. Let the beans cook down until some fall apart and the liquid gets soupy. Add more water if they get too dry. Serve with corn bread.

Ingredients

1 pound crowders
  Water to cover
3 cloves garlic, peeled
2 bay leaves
2 teaspoons salt
  Dash cayenne pepper
  Dash white pepper
1 tablespoon olive oil
1 onion, chopped
½ head green cabbage, roughly
    chopped
2 to 3 large fresh tomatoes
1 quart water
2 teaspoons salt
  Black pepper to taste
½ can beer
½ bunch fresh parsley
4 scallions, thinly sliced

CROWDER PEA AND CABBAGE STEW

Crowder peas look like black-eyes, but their eyes aren't black. To me, they taste a little "greener" than black-eyes. Crowders can be cooked just like fresh limas or black-eyes. Vary the time depending on the freshness and size of the pea. Here's a summer stew featuring crowders.

SERVES 6.

Preparation

Rinse the crowders, place in a heavy pot, and cover by 2 inches with cold water. Add the garlic cloves, bay leaves, salt, cayenne, and white pepper and bring to a boil. Skim the foam that rises up, stir the peas, turn down the heat a little, and cook until they're just tender. Drain, reserving the garlic and bay leaves.

Place the pot back on the stove and heat the olive oil. Add the onion and cook on high for about 4 minutes. Meanwhile, mince the reserved cooked garlic cloves and add to the pot. Add the cabbage and cook on high for about 3 or 4 minutes. Stir in the crowders along with the bay leaves and the chopped tomatoes. Cook about 3 minutes, stirring. Add the water and the additional salt and pepper. Bring to a boil. Stir, reduce the heat to medium, and cook, stirring occasionally, for about 15 minutes. Add the beer and cook 10 more minutes. Add the parsley and scallions, and continue to cook. You want the crowders tender, but not falling apart. The sauce should be somewhat thickened.

Taste and adjust the seasoning. Discard the bay leaves. Serve as a side, or as a meal over a bowl of rice or mashed potatoes.

BLACK-EYED PEAS (HOPPIN' JOHN)

You must have these on New Year's Day. A whole year's luck depends upon it, and a whole day's eating satisfaction.

SERVES 6 TO 8.

Ingredients

- 1 pound fresh or dried black-eyed peas
- 2 tablespoons butter
- 1 yellow onion, diced
- 2 stalks celery, diced
- 1 green bell pepper, diced
- 2½ quarts chicken stock
- 1 tablespoon salt
- 1 teaspoon black pepper
- 2 dried cayenne peppers
- 1 bay leaf
- 1 cup long grain rice
- ½ yellow onion, diced
   Hot sauce

Preparation

If using dried peas (which you will be doing in January, in this hemisphere at least) rinse and sort, and soak overnight in water. If using fresh, rinse and sort through. Set aside. Melt the butter in a heavy soup stock pot and cook the onion, celery, and bell pepper just to wilt. Add the stock and bring to a boil. Add the peas, salt, pepper, cayenne, and bay leaf. Return to a boil and skim any scum that rises to the top. Reduce the heat to medium low and cook until the peas are just tender, about 1 hour for dried peas and 15 minutes for fresh.

Add the rice and stir well. Cover and cook for 15 more minutes, or until the rice is done and the stock is absorbed. Discard the bay leaf.

Serve with raw chopped onion and vinegar hot sauce such as Crystal or Red Rooster.

2   pounds fresh Brussels sprouts

2   quarts water

2   teaspoons salt

¼   cup butter

2   scallions, thinly sliced

     Zest and juice of 1 lemon

     Salt and white pepper to taste

BRUSSELS SPROUTS WITH BROWN BUTTER

I crave these in the fall. They go great with roasted turkey or flavorful game like rabbit.

SERVES 6 TO 8.

Preparation

Trim the ends of the Brussels sprouts and cut in half lengthwise. Pour the water into a saucepan and bring to a boil with the salt. Add the Brussel sprouts and cook until tender but not mushy, about 7 minutes. Drain the Brussels sprouts. Heat the butter in a heavy skillet and add the sprouts and scallions, tossing to coat. Carefully allow the butter to brown, not burn. Add the lemon juice, zest, and salt and pepper as desired. Serve immediately.

BOILED CABBAGE WITH BUTTER

I really, really love this cabbage. It's probably my ultimate comfort food. I think I like boiled cabbage best on crisp evenings in early spring when my senses demand something green that will still warm my bones. I almost always serve it with Garlic Mashed Potatoes (see recipe, page 85). In fact, I'm divinely happy with a big soup bowl filled with just those two.

SERVES 10.

Ingredients

- 1   head green cabbage
- 3   quarts water
- ¼   cup butter
- 1   tablespoon salt
- 1   teaspoon cracked black pepper
- 1   pod dried cayenne pepper
     Juice of 2 lemons

Preparation

Core the cabbage and roughly chop. Place in a pot and cover with water. Add butter, salt, and peppers, and bring to a boil. Reduce the heat and cook on low about 15 or so minutes until cooked but still slightly firm. Add lemon juice, adjust the seasonings, and serve.

BRAISED RED CABBAGE

I love this with fried pork chops or sausages. A great cold-weather vegetable.

SERVES 10.

Ingredients

- 1   head red cabbage
- 1   small red onion, thinly sliced
- 1   tablespoon vegetable oil
- ½   cup red wine
- ¼   cup red wine vinegar
- 1   tablespoon firmly packed brown sugar
- 1   teaspoon juniper berries
- 1   teaspoon salt
- ½   teaspoon white pepper
- ½   teaspoon celery seeds

Preparation

Core the cabbage and slice thinly. Heat the oil in a deep skillet or Dutch oven. Add the onion and sauté over fairly high heat until the onion is translucent. Add the cabbage and toss to coat well with the oil. Sauté until the cabbage is wilted. Add the wine, vinegar, brown sugar, juniper berries, salt, and pepper. Stir well and cover. Turn the heat to low and cook for about 15 to 20 minutes. Remove from the heat and stir in the celery seeds.

This is a marvelous bed for pork chops or rabbit, or even venison roasts.

Ingredients

1   head green cabbage, cored
2   quarts salted water
½   pound loose pork sausage
1   onion, small dice
3   cloves garlic, minced
2   ribs celery, finely diced
1   carrot, finely diced
2   cups raw white rice
3   cups chicken stock
1   teaspoon red pepper flakes
1   bay leaf
1   teaspoon fresh sage, minced
1   teaspoon fresh thyme leaves
2   scallions, thinly sliced
1   tablespoon fresh chopped
     parsley
     Salt, if needed (the sausage
     is quite salty)
2   cups chicken stock

STUFFED CABBAGE

There are a million ways to stuff cabbage. My favorite, and I believe the most traditional Southern way, is with rice and pork sausage. This is a most satisfying supper on a blustery winter's eve.

MAKES ABOUT 12 STUFFED CABBAGE LEAVES.

Preparation

Remove and separate the large individual cabbage leaves. Bring the water to a simmer in a wide shallow pot and drop the cabbage leaves in until they wilt and become pliable, about 5 minutes. Drain on paper towels.

Cook the sausage in a deep skillet, breaking up the meat as it cooks. When the sausage is about halfway done add the onion, garlic, and celery, and cook with the sausage for about 5 minutes. Add the carrot and continue cooking a couple of minutes. Stir in the raw rice and cook for 2 minutes. Add 3 cups of stock, bring to a boil, and reduce to simmer. Add the pepper flakes and bay leaf. Cover and cook for about 10 minutes, until rice is about two thirds done. Remove from the heat and cool. Stir in the fresh herbs and adjust the seasoning.

Preheat the oven to 400°. Remove any very thick ribs from the cabbage leaves. Lay the cabbage leaves flat and, depending on the leaf size, place about 2 or 3 tablespoons of filling one third of the way up the center of the leaf. Roll the bottom third over the filling, fold over the sides, and roll up, not too tight. Fill remaining leaves in the same manner. Place the stuffed leaves in a Dutch oven and pour the remaining 2 cups of stock over. Cover the Dutch oven with a lid and bake for 20 to 30 minutes, until the rice is completely done. Serve with a little rich Tomato Sauce (see recipe, page 113).

COPPER PENNY CARROTS

These look very pretty on a plate in the winter when the vegetables tend to not inspire.

SERVES 6.

2   quarts water

2   teaspoons salt

1   pound young carrots, peeled and sliced in thin coins

½   yellow onion, sliced in thin circles

3   tablespoons butter

¼   cup firmly packed brown sugar

1   teaspoon chopped fresh parsley

Preparation

Bring the water to a boil with the salt. Add the remaining ingredients except the parsley. Turn the heat to medium and allow the liquid to reduce as the carrots cook. Watch so that they don't cook too quickly and scorch. Add a little more water if necessary. When the carrots are cooked, the liquid, butter, and sugar should be cooked down to a syrupy glaze. Sprinkle with chopped parsley and serve.

Ingredients

1 tablespoon salt

1 pound small shell pasta

1 tablespoon butter

2 eggs

1½ cups milk (or cream)

1 teaspoon ground black
   pepper

12 ounces sharp Cheddar
   cheese, grated
   Paprika

MACARONI AND CHEESE

Catherine Couch, my grandmother's housekeeper, made the best in the world, heavy on the black pepper. I always got in trouble for picking off the crispy pieces on top.

SERVES 6.

Preparation

Preheat the oven to 365°. Fill a large pot with water and the tablespoon of salt and bring to a boil. Pour in the pasta, stirring, and cook about 6 minutes, until slightly undercooked. Drain and run under cold water.

Place the pasta in a 2-quart casserole and toss with the butter to keep it from sticking. Beat together the eggs, milk or cream, and pepper, and pour over the pasta. Add three-fourths of the cheese and mix together. Sprinkle the rest of the cheese on top and then the paprika. Cover with foil and bake for 30 minutes. Remove the foil and turn the broiler on to brown the top. Lightly brown and serve before someone, usually me, steals all of the browned pieces from the top.

2 tablespoons butter

2 tablespoons all-purpose
   flour

1 cup milk
   Dash white pepper
   Dash red pepper

1½ cups grated cheese

3 eggs, separated

CHEESE SOUFFLÉ

This makes a very nice luncheon or light supper with a spinach salad and a glass of wine. You could get some really different flavors by varying the type of cheese. Cheddar is about all that's been around for the last several decades, and a good sharp Cheddar works great, but a goat cheese or something aged would make it an entirely different dish.

SERVES 6 TO 8.

Preparation

Preheat the oven to 300°. Grease a soufflé dish or casserole. Place butter in the top of a double boiler and melt over simmering water. Stir in the flour and cook a few minutes, and then add the milk and peppers. Cook for several minutes, then stir in the grated cheese. Beat the egg yolks and stir in. Let cook until thickened. Remove from the heat and let cool slightly. Beat the egg whites stiff and fold in. Spoon into the casserole and bake for 30 minutes, until risen and lightly browned.

Ingredients

8	ears field corn
1/2	to 1 cup milk, if needed
1/4	cup butter (or 3 tablespoons bacon grease)
2	teaspoons salt
1	teaspoon fresh ground black pepper

FRIED CORN

Fried corn as known in Middle Tennessee is not actually fried, but rather stewed with butter or bacon grease and its own milky liquid. Daddy is a master at fried corn. He's liberal with the black pepper, and he can wait to stir the corn until just the right moment when you get some yummy, chewy kind of crusty thing going on underneath. Daddy and I both much prefer tougher field corn to the tender and sweeter Silver Queen for this particular dish. Field corn has a nice toothsomeness to it and furthermore, Silver Queen is sometimes just too blame sweet for me.

SERVES 8.

Preparation

Shuck and clean the corn and cut the kernels from the cob. Use your knife to scrape down the cob, milking it of all of its juice. If the corn doesn't have much milk, you may put the corn in a bowl, pouring about a half cup of true milk over it. Heat the fat in a cast-iron skillet. Add the corn with the milk, salt, and pepper. Stir once and let the corn sit on medium high heat for several minutes before stirring or turning again. If the mixture seems too dry, add a little more milk, but you don't want it too runny, either. Turn the heat down to low and let it cook, stirring occasionally, for about 20 minutes.

CORN PUDDING WITH SAGE

I love the fresh sage with the corn and cheese. It makes this a really rich tasting dish. I don't recommend using dried sage. Sage is a semi-evergreen, and my sage stays green for a good ten months a year. It's very easy to grow and gets huge in a couple of years. Its pretty purple flowers make a great garnish, too.

SERVES 6.

Ingredients

- 4 ears corn
- 1 tablespoon butter
- 1/2 yellow onion, diced
- 1/2 green bell pepper, diced
- 1 teaspoon salt
- 1/4 teaspoon cayenne pepper
- 1/2 teaspoon black pepper
- 1/4 cup cornmeal
- 2 1/2 cups milk
- 2 eggs, beaten
- 2 teaspoons fresh sage, minced
- 1/2 cup Parmesan or other hard cheese, grated

Preparation

Shuck and clean the corn and remove the kernels from the cob, scraping to remove milky liquid from the cob. Set the kernels with the liquid aside. Heat the butter in a deep skillet and sauté the onion for 3 minutes. Add the bell pepper and cook for 5 more minutes. Add the seasoning and cornmeal, and stir. Add the milk, stirring. Let the mixture cook 5 minutes, until thickened. Mix in the corn and liquid. Remove the skillet from the heat and stir in the beaten eggs, sage, and all but 2 tablespoons of the cheese. Pour the mixture into a casserole. Make a steam bath by setting the casserole inside a slightly larger pan, filled halfway with hot water. Bake at 350° until the pudding is almost set, about 35 minutes.

Sprinkle with the remaining 2 tablespoons of cheese and cook for another 10 or so minutes until firm and browned on top. Serve hot.

Ingredients

6 ears corn
½ cup butter, softened
   Salt and pepper to taste

ROASTED OR GRILLED CORN

This cooking method really intensifies the rich sweet flavor of corn, and the grilled version adds a nice smokiness.

SERVES 6.

Preparation

Preheat the oven to 425° or light the grill. Pull the shucks down from the corn cobs, not removing them. Remove the the silks. Spread a teaspoon or two of the butter over the corn kernels and sprinkle with salt and pepper if desired. Pull the shucks back up over the ears and tie with twine to secure. Place the ears of corn on indirect heat on the grill or directly onto the racks of the oven and cook the corn, turning occasionally on the grill for 30 minutes. Remove the husks and serve with additional butter and seasoning.

Grits

Many old cookbooks refer to grits as hominy. If you look at a package of grits closely, you'll see that most actually say "hominy grits." Hominy refers to the fact that the corn is dried and hulled. Grits are then ground.

To my fancy cosmopolitan friends, I explain that grits are simply polenta, the trendy Italian corn-mash generally made with white corn instead of yellow. Like polenta, grits are incredibly versatile. They can be cooked stove top and served creamy, usually the way you have them for breakfast with your eggs. You can also mix them with seasoning and cheese and bake them, or you can spread the hot grits in a shallow baking dish, chill it, cut out the grits in shapes and pan fry it.

Like all cereals, creamy grits need to be highly seasoned to taste worth a damn. To most Southerners this means salt, black pepper, and maybe a little hot sauce, plus plenty of butter. Then, of course, you scrape your bacon or country ham in them, break in your fried egg, and kind of mush the whole thing around a bit in your own personal style. This is actually what makes grits taste good. I have known those who ate sweetened grits as you would cream of wheat, but you don't see it too often and I can't say I recommend the practice.

SIMPLE GRITS

4   cups water
1   teaspoon salt
1   cup grits (not quick cook-
    ing)
1   tablespoon butter (or more)

SERVES 4.

Preparation

Bring the salted water to boil in a saucepan and stir in the grits. Turn the heat down to medium and cook the grits, stirring until very thick, about 20 minutes. Serve with butter, salt, and pepper.

Grits marked "quick grits" are a lot like quick oatmeal. They take about 10 minutes less time and seem to be something that a lot of us have gotten used to. A tasting of the slow-cooking variety (preferably from a small operation such as Nora Mill in northern Georgia) will remind you of how grits are supposed to taste.

CHEESE GRITS

2   tablespoons butter
1/2 onion, chopped
3   cups water
1/2 teaspoon salt
1/4 teaspoon black pepper
    Dash cayenne pepper
1   cup grits
1/2 cup grated sharp Cheddar
    cheese

For people who think they don't like grits. I defy them all. For cheese grits with even more seasoning, look at the recipe for Patty Pan Squash with Cheese Grits (see recipe, page 93).

SERVES 4.

Preparation

Melt the butter in a saucepan and add the onion. Cook about 3 minutes, then pour in the water with the salt and pepper and bring to a boil. Stir in the grits. Turn the heat down to medium, and cook until thickened, around 2 minutes, stirring constantly. Stir in the cheese and pour into a buttered casserole. Bake at 350° for about 30 minutes until heated through and browned on top.

1   28-ounce can white hominy
1   tablespoon olive oil
½   yellow onion, diced
3   cloves garlic, minced
2   ripe tomatoes, diced
1   teaspoon salt
¼   teaspoon cayenne pepper
¼   teaspoon paprika
¼   teaspoon black pepper
     Juice of ½ lemon

SEASONED HOMINY

Hominy is corn that has had the hull removed. Rather a strange idea, particularly when you realize that lye is used in the processing. Regardless, hominy is a mainstay in Southern and in Mexican cooking. Grits are actually ground from hominy. Canned hominy is a wonderful addition to stews and soups, or a very tasty side dish with just a little jazzing up.

SERVES 4.

Preparation

Drain and rinse the hominy. Set aside. Heat the oil in a skillet. Add the onion and cook 3 minutes. Add the garlic and cook 1 more minute. Add the tomatoes, salt, and peppers, and stir. Let cook about 10 minutes, until the tomatoes are beginning to dry out. Add the hominy to the pan and cook just to heat through, about 5 minutes. Stir in the lemon juice and serve.

SAUTÉED CUCUMBER

The trick to cooking cucumbers is to cook them lightly or the texture becomes ugly and the flavor nonexistent. I think perhaps that this concept of light application is difficult for us who were raised with mainly bland vegetables picked under-ripe and shipped across country. We're so used to adding lots of seasoning or heavy sauces in an attempt to give flavor to the flavorless that it's hard for us to allow a beautiful, simple thing to be simply beautiful. My goodness, such a sermon.

SERVES 4.

Ingredients

2   teaspoons butter
2   very fresh cucumbers, sliced
1   teaspoon minced chervil or
     tarragon
     Dash salt and white pepper
     Juice of 1/4 lemon

Preparation

Warm the butter in a skillet to just sizzling and toss in the cucumber, shaking the pan to coat the slices. Cook quickly on high heat for 3 or 4 minutes, until the cucumbers are heated through and slightly wilted. Add the remaining ingredients, toss well, and serve immediately.

Eggplant

Eggplant is another vegetable that lingered near obscurity in the South for the greater part of this century. My parents ate eggplant as children, but my first impression of eggplant was of some exotic, threateningly obscene novelty which I would see at the County Fair. The only thing I could figure out that people did with eggplant was to try to grow the biggest one and win a blue ribbon from 4H. My real romance with eggplant began in my late teens and hasn't faltered yet. Some day I would love to write an entire book extolling the virtues of eggplant, so I won't risk boring you here. Just let me say that eggplant is as happy to be in the South as Southerners are happy to eat it. Eggplant does phenomenally well in our hot and humid summers. It's the perfect vegetable for a novice gardener to plant, or a good one to find at farmers' markets and vegetable stands. Look for some heirloom varieties that are different colors and shapes.

Ingredients

- 1/4 cup olive oil
- 1 yellow onion, diced medium
- 1 eggplant, the skin scored and diced large
- 1 green bell pepper, chopped
- 1 red bell pepper, chopped
- 1 pint mushrooms, quartered (optional)
- 4 ripe tomatoes, peeled and roughly chopped
- 5 cloves garlic, minced
- 2 tablespoons red wine vinegar
- 1 teaspoon fresh thyme leaves
- 1 teaspoon summer savory (optional)
- 1 tablespoon salt
- 2 teaspoons black pepper
- 1/2 teaspoon red pepper flakes

STEWED EGGPLANT

SERVES 8.

Preparation

Heat the oil in a Dutch oven. Add the onion and cook 5 minutes. Add the eggplant and cook 5 more minutes. Add the peppers, garlic, and mushrooms, and cook 5 minutes. Add the tomatoes and cook 5 more minutes. Add the remaining ingredients and cook over medium for 20 to 30 minutes.

My grandmother served this as one of the many vegetable dishes that appeared on the dinner table. Stewed eggplant is great over rice or pasta or pour it into a casserole, top with breadcrumbs and a little fresh goat cheese, and bake. Serve as a main dish with a salad and some bread.

FRIED EGGPLANT

Eggplant is so good like this. Crispy coating and smooth and savory inside. Serve it with fresh lemon, or maybe a little tomato sauce.

The only problem I have with this recipe is that I have a tendency to eat most of the eggplant before I can get it to the table. Consider doubling the recipe.

SERVES 6.

Ingredients

1 large eggplant
3 eggs
¾ cup dry breadcrumbs
¼ teaspoon cayenne pepper
¼ teaspoon black pepper
¼ teaspoon garlic powder
½ teaspoon dried oregano
½ cup vegetable oil
 Salt to taste

Preparation

Peel the eggplant and cut into finger-size pieces. Sprinkle heavily with salt and place in a colander to drain for 1 hour. This rids the eggplant of any bitter juices. Press lightly on the eggplant to drain. Beat the eggs. Mix the breadcrumbs with the seasonings and place in a plate. Drop the eggplant fingers in the egg and roll each in the bread crumbs to coat. Place coated fingers on a baking sheet and place in the freezer for 15 minutes. This makes the breading adhere.

In a deep skillet heat the oil to 325° or almost smoking. Fry the chilled eggplant fingers a few at a time until browned on all sides. Drain on clean brown paper bags. Sprinkle with salt and serve hot.

Greens

Hooray for greens! Let them be heralded among the noble vegetables and in the voices and hearts of man! Greens are one of the foods for which my body physically yearns and aches. When I was pregnant with my daughter and bordering on anemia, I practically ate my weight in greens: turnips, mustard, collards, kale, and an occasional bowl of poke salet. Greens to me taste like life itself, pungent, vibrant, and and full of pepper. I especially love greens in the cool months of spring when I need a tonic from the winter and again in autumn when my blood begins to race with the prospect of first frost. These are the best seasons for greens, the shoots are young and tender and the flavor more teasing than it is bold.

Other than poke salet, which is in a class all its own, I have two ways of cooking all varieties of greens. The first is purely traditional with salty ham and pepper. My own "newfangled" recipe for greens upsets purists like my father, until they take their first bite. I haven't missed a convert yet.

OLD-FASHIONED GREENS

In tough times, this would be the extent of many Southern suppers, along with some corn bread to mop up the "licker." I'm sure it made tough times a little less tough. Now it is usually one of several vegetables offered with dinner. Hot sauce would be greatly appreciated with this fine dish.

SERVES 8.

Ingredients

- 4 bunches greens (kale, collard, mustard, turnip, or dandelion)
- ½ pound country ham trimmings (or a meaty bone)
- 4 or more dried whole cayennes
- 1 gallon water
- 1 to 2 teaspoons salt, or to taste

Preparation

Pick the greens well, removing the tough stems, and wash very well in a couple or even several changes of cold water, if necessary. Fill a large pot with water and add the ham hock. Bring to a boil and cook for 20 minutes before adding the greens and salt. Remember, the pork is already salty. Bring back to a boil, reduce the heat, and cook until quite tender, an hour or more.

Note: Some people like to soak their dandelion greens in ice water for an hour before cooking to remove some of the bitterness. Picking only the youngest greens will avoid this problem.

GREENS WITH TOMATOES

SERVES 6.

2 bunches greens
1/4 cup olive oil
1 yellow or white onion, thinly sliced
3 cloves garlic, minced
1 25-ounce can tomatoes
2 cups plus water
 Salt to taste (start with 1½ teaspoons)
 Black pepper to taste
 Several squirts hot sauce
1 tablespoon malt vinegar

Preparation

Clean the greens well and wash in several changes of cold water, as necessary. Drain. Heat the oil in a stock pot and sauté the onion and garlic. Toss in the greens and stir until wilted. Add the tomatoes and their juice, squeezing the tomatoes to break them up. Add the remaining ingredients and bring to a boil. Reduce the heat to medium and cook for 45 or so minutes, until the greens are tender but not mushy. You may need to add a little water. Adjust the seasoning to taste. Serve with corn bread and additional hot sauce and vinegar. This will clean your insides out and wake the sleepiest of taste buds.

POKE SALET

Poke salet is very rarely seen in the grocery store, but it is seen in every yard in which I have ever mucked about in Middle Tennessee. The berries of the plant are poisonous, and even the leaves really must be long cooked or they'll upset most stomachs. If the plant gets too large, the greens will be frighteningly bitter, but the young leaves are simply, shall we say, pronounced in flavor.

Preparation

Clean the greens well and cook as in the above old-fashioned greens recipe, with maybe a little less water. When the greens are done, after a couple of hours, drain off about 2 cups. Heat a little bacon fat in a skillet. Stir in the greens and 3 beaten eggs. Scramble together.

This is a feast served with Hot Water Corn Bread (see recipe, page 153) and a vinegar pepper sauce.

Okra

Okra is a sacred vegetable in the South and throughout the Caribbean. Africans brought okra seeds with them across the ocean on the heinous slave ships. A seed of hope and life amongst so much horror.

Okra grows like a weed in our hot and muggy summers. The only difficulty with growing okra here is catching the vegetable while it is still small and tender. They mature very quickly becoming woody and tough. Do yourself and your friends a favor and only prepare small okra, even for frying and stews. The smallest ones are delightful fried whole.

Ingredients

- 1 cup cornmeal
- 1/2 teaspoon garlic powder
- 1/2 teaspoon salt
- 1/4 teaspoon cayenne pepper
- 1/4 teaspoon black pepper
- 1 cup buttermilk
- 1 pound okra, (leave 1-inch okra whole, cut in 1/2-inch slices)
- 1/2 cup vegetable oil

FRIED OKRA

SERVES 4.

Preparation

Mix the dry ingredients in a bowl. Pour the buttermilk into another bowl. Clean and prep the okra and place in the buttermilk. Lift the okra from the buttermilk with a slotted spoon and roll in the cornmeal mixture. When the pieces are well covered, place them on a plate or baking sheet and put in the freezer for 15 minutes to set the coating. Heat the oil in an iron skillet to 325° or just below smoking. Add the okra to the hot oil and cook for 5 to 7 minutes, turning to brown on all sides. Drain on paper towels, sprinkle with salt, and serve hot.

¼ cup olive oil

1 yellow onion, diced medium

3 cloves garlic, minced

1 or 2 banana peppers, cut in ½-inch slices

1 pound okra (leave small okra whole, otherwise cut into ½- or 1-inch slices)

½ pound small tender okra, stem ends trimmed

1 teaspoon salt

1 teaspoon black pepper

¼ teaspoon red pepper flakes (optional)

2 fresh tomatoes, peeled (optional) and roughly chopped

2 tablespoons red wine vinegar

2 scallions, sliced (optional)

STEWED OKRA

Tastes like the glories of summer. I can't get enough.

SERVES 6.

Preparation

Heat the oil in a heavy skillet and sauté the onion for 3 minutes. Add the garlic and peppers and cook 2 more minutes. Add the okra, salt, and peppers, and cook 5 minutes. Add the tomato and cook on medium high for about 5 minutes, until a little dry. Add the vinegar and cook another 5 minutes. Stir, reduce the heat to low, and cook another 5 or 10 minutes, until the okra is very tender. Sprinkle with sliced scallions, if you like, and serve hot. This is a meal over rice, or just one of the many vegetable dishes to laden a Southern dinner table.

I have heard some misguided souls complain about the "slimy texture" of okra. I myself find the texture more luxurious than slimy, however I will note that leaving the okra whole will hold in most of its juices, greatly alleviating the "slime factor."

Ingredients

6 yellow onions (Vidalia, if in
   season)
  Water
2 teaspoons salt
1 cup breadcrumbs
1/2 tablespoon salt
1/4 teaspoon black pepper
2 teaspoons fresh thyme leaves
1 cup butter
1 cup heavy cream
1/4 cup Parmesan cheese

SCALLOPED ONIONS

Rich and savory, serve them with a simple roast.

SERVES 6 TO 8.

Preparation

Preheat the oven to 350°. Slice the onions about 1-inch thick. Place in a heavy pot with about 1 inch of water to cover them. Add the salt and bring to a boil. Cover, reduce the heat to low, and cook for 15 minutes or so until the onions are tender. Add a little more water, if necessary, to keep the onions covered. Drain the onions and place in a baking dish, layering with a sprinkle of breadcrumbs, a little salt and pepper, and thyme, and dotting with pieces of butter. Place the last layer of onions and pour the cream over. Top with breadcrumbs and Parmesan, and bake for 30 to 40 minutes until bubbly and browned on top.

Ingredients

3 yellow onions
1/4 cup butter
1 tablespoon firmly packed
   brown sugar
2 teaspoons salt
1/2 teaspoon white pepper
1/4 cup red wine vinegar

GLAZED ONIONS

Wonderful with a hundred dishes. The perfect "sauce" for simply grilled meat, the classic with fried calf's liver. This makes an awesome "bed" for grilled fish or chicken or an intriguing topping for a green salad.

SERVES 6.

Preparation

Thinly slice the onions. Heat the butter in a cast-iron skillet and add the brown sugar, stirring to dissolve. Add the onions with the salt and pepper, stirring. Cook the onions on medium high until they are translucent. Turn the heat to low and cook slowly for 1 hour or so, stirring occasionally to avoid burning. Turn heat back to high and, when the pan starts to sizzle, pour in the vinegar, stirring constantly. Cook for a few more minutes, until the vinegar is syrupy.

ONION SOUFFLÉ

A hearty tasting dish for a blustery, dark night.

SERVES 6 TO 8.

- ¼ cup butter
- 4 large yellow onions, finely chopped
- Salt to taste
- ½ teaspoon white pepper
- 2 teaspoons minced fresh sage
- 3 tablespoons all-purpose flour
- 1 cup milk
- ¼ cup grated cheese (something twangy like a fresh goat or yogurt cheese)
- 5 egg whites
- ½ teaspoon cream of tartar

Preparation

Preheat the oven to 350°. Heat 2 tablespoons of the butter in a skillet and cook the onions on medium high until translucent. Reduce the heat and simmer on low, stirring occasionally, for about 15 minutes. Transfer the mixture to a food processor or blender and purée. Season with salt, pepper, and sage, and set aside. You should have about 2 cups.

Heat the remaining butter in a saucepan and stir in the flour to a smooth consistency. Cook on medium for about 5 minutes, stirring constantly.

Meanwhile, heat the milk slightly. Pour the milk into the roux, whisking out any lumps. Bring the sauce to a slight boil. Turn the heat to low and cook, stirring occasionally, for 10 minutes. Add the onion, stir well, and cook another 10 minutes. Add the cheese and stir until melted. Remove from the heat and let the mixture cool.

Beat the egg whites until almost stiff. Sprinkle the cream of tartar over the egg whites and continue to beat until stiff. Gently fold the egg whites into the onion mixture, careful not to over mix. Pour into a 3-quart soufflé dish and bake for about 30 minutes, until risen and browned on top. Serve immediately.

ONION RINGS

Who can resist? Crispy, sweet, and savory. And these are the best.

SERVES 6.

Ingredients

- 4 yellow onions
- 1 cup all-purpose flour
- 1 tablespoon salt
- 1 teaspoon black pepper
- 3 cups buttermilk
- 4 cups vegetable oil
- 2 cups cornmeal
- 1 tablespoon salt
- 1 teaspoon cayenne

Preparation

Peel the onions and slice ½-inch thin. Place the flour in a large bowl. Stir the salt and black pepper in with the flour. Pour in the buttermilk and mix. Separate the onions into rings and drop into the batter. Refrigerate the batter with the onion rings in it for an hour.

Heat the oil to 325° or just under smoking. Place the cornmeal on a plate and stir in the salt and pepper. Lift the onion rings from the batter and dredge in the cornmeal before frying. Fry about 5 minutes, turning, until golden brown. Drain on clean paper bags, sprinkle with salt, and serve.

Parsnips

Oh, pity the poor parsnip. Once so highly regaled and fondly munched upon, now we can scarcely find the fellow in the grocery store. And, if you do find a parsnip, chances are very good that it will be encased in a thick wax coating to maximize its shelf life. Of course I have been told many times that the wax is not toxic and that you can chip the wax away. I say who wants wax of any form, toxic or non, coating their insides or mucking up their kitchen table and floor. Please, take a stand and tell your grocer that you simply don't want wax. Perhaps, if we all bend their ears, the farmers will hear and the parsnip may once again bask in its own naked beauty.

We must do our part by eating lots and lots of parsnips at a suitable rate of consumption so that they do not rot on the grocery store shelves. And what a delightful task. In case you're not familiar, a parsnip is carrot-like in shape and slightly turnip-like in taste. Parsnips become sweeter after the temperature drops to forty degrees for several hours or days, even, making them a cold weather vegetable. The texture when cooked may range from slightly firm to mashed and puréed. Parsnips add a new depth to stews or pot pies, and a wonderful twangy richness to mashed potatoes. Parsnip recipes were all over cook books from the last century, but like so many vegetables of character, were somehow streamlined out of vogue. I do see parsnips popping up in more cook's magazines and on trendy menus these days, so hopefully the parsnip's days of obscurity are numbered.

BUTTERED PARSNIPS

Ingredients

6 large parsnips
Water to cover
2 teaspoons salt
1 teaspoon white pepper
1 bay leaf
1 tablespoon butter
1 tablespoon minced fresh
 parsley

SERVES 6.

Preparation

Peel the parsnips and slice in discs, halving and quartering the discs as the parsnip widens, to get pieces of relatively the same size. Place the parsnips in a saucepan, cover with water, and add the salt, pepper, and bay leaf. Bring to a boil. Reduce the heat to medium and cook the parsnips until tender, about 10 minutes. Drain the parsnips, discard the bay leaf, and return to the pan along with the butter. Shake the pan until the butter is melted. Add the parsley and shake the pan to coat the parsnips. Check seasoning for salt and pepper and serve immediately.

SCALLOPED PARSNIPS

Very old cook books frequently call for bacon with parsnips. The smoky flavor is a satisfying match to the pungency of parsnips. Not many of us cook with bacon grease these days for numerous and obvious reasons. However, if you feel like throwing caution to wind, this is a good place to do so.

SERVES 6.

Ingredients

1 tablespoon butter (or bacon grease)

½ yellow onion, thinly sliced

6 large parsnips
  Water to cover

2 teaspoons salt

½ cup shredded strong white Cheddar or blue cheese

½ cup cream

½ cup toasted breadcrumbs

1 tablespoon chopped fresh parsley
  Dash cayenne or paprika

Preparation

Preheat the oven to 350°. Heat the butter or bacon grease in a skillet and cook the onions for about 5 minutes until translucent,. Peel the parsnips and cut lengthwise in ½-inch thick slices. Place the parsnips in a pot and cover with water. Add salt and bring to a boil. Reduce the heat to medium and barely cook through the parsnips, about 3 or 4 minutes. Drain the parsnips. Place half in a casserole, scattering half the onions over. Sprinkle about a fourth of the cheese over. Repeat with one more layer, and pour cream over. Sprinkle breadcrumbs and the remaining cheese on top. Top with a dash of cayenne or paprika. Cover with foil and bake for 20 minutes.

Remove the foil and place back in the oven for 10 more minutes. Sprinkle parsley over and serve hot.

Peas

Fresh peas are a great luxury. It takes a lot of time to shell them, with a fairly low yield. Think of it as therapy. Shelling peas will force you to slow down. A rocking chair is nice place to sit while shelling and a front or back porch is a nice place for the rocking chair. A friend or relation is a nice person to shell with, but not a necessity. You'll probably find yourself humming a little tune if you shell alone. And what rewards! A fresh pea is an altogether different creature from the canned or frozen version. Fresh peas are as delicate and flirtatious as spring itself. Leave the processed peas for stews and pot pies. Fresh peas should be simply cooked.

Ingredients

- 4 cups fresh shelled peas
  Water to cover
- 2 teaspoons salt
- ½ teaspoon white pepper
- ¼ cup butter
- 1 tablespoon fresh mint,
  roughly chopped

FRESH PEAS WITH BUTTER AND MINT

Perhaps the best way to serve those little green pearls, so that the flavor can really shine through.

SERVES 6.

Preparation

Rinse and clean the peas. Place in a pot and cover with water. Add salt and pepper and bring to a boil. Reduce the heat to medium and cook about 10 to 15 minutes until the peas are tender but not mushy. Drain the peas and return to the pot with the butter, shaking the pan until the butter melts. Add mint and toss to coat. Serve immediately.

PEAS AND CARROTS WITH CREAM

A very pretty, delicate tasting spring vegetable. Lovely with roasted chicken or lamb.

SERVES 6.

Ingredients

3 cups fresh shelled peas
2 carrots, diced
   Water to cover
2 teaspoons salt
1 teaspoon white pepper
1 bay leaf
1 pint cream
¼ onion, minced
1 tablespoon minced fresh dill

Preparation

Rinse and clean the peas. Place in a pot with the diced carrots. Cover with water and add the salt, pepper, and bay leaf. Bring to a boil. Reduce the heat to medium high and cook about 10 minutes until tender. Drain. Meanwhile, pour the cream into a saucepan with the onion and bring to a simmer. Simmer until the cream is reduced by half. Place the peas and carrots back in the saucepan and add the reduced cream. Stir and place on the stove until the vegetables are heated. Stir in the dill and serve immediately.

CREOLE SHRIMP-STUFFED PEPPERS

A beautiful entree you can make in advance. Serve them with rich Tomato Sauce (see recipe, page 113).

SERVES 6 AS THE MAIN COURSE.

Ingredients

- 6 large green bell peppers
- 3 tablespoons vegetable oil
- ½ yellow onion, diced
- 3 cloves garlic, minced
- 2 ribs celery, diced
- ½ red bell pepper, diced

- 1½ cups white rice
- 1 teaspoon salt
- ½ teaspoon black pepper
- ¼ teaspoon cayenne pepper
- ¼ teaspoon paprika
- 1 bay leaf
- 3 cups chicken or vegetable stock
- 1 pound small shrimp, shelled
- 1 teaspoon fresh minced rosemary
- 1 teaspoon minced fresh thyme
- 1 teaspoon minced fresh basil
- 1 tablespoon dry breadcrumbs
- 1 tablespoon minced fresh parsley
- 1 tablespoon minced scallions

Preparation

Cut the tops off of the peppers and clean out the ribs and seeds from the inside. Bring a pot of salted water to boil and parboil the peppers about 3 minutes. Drain and reserve. Heat the oil in a deep skillet and cook the onion until translucent. Add the garlic, celery, and bell pepper, and cook about 5 minutes. Add the rice and stir, cooking until rice is pearly looking. Add the salt, peppers, paprika, bay leaf, and stock. Bring to a boil, stirring well. Cover, reduce the heat, and simmer for 10 minutes. Remove the lid and lightly stir in the shrimp, fresh rosemary, thyme, and basil. Cover and continue cooking for 5 more minutes. Remove from the stove and let cool.

Preheat the oven to 375°. Taste the stuffing and adjust the seasoning to suit your taste. Generously fill each pepper with the stuffing (any leftover stuffing may be saved and used to stuff trout, squash, tomatoes, onions, mushrooms, or eggplant, or simply eaten on its own). Sprinkle the top of each pepper with breadcrumbs, then parsley and scallions. Bake uncovered for 20 minutes until heated through and brown on top.

Mashed Potatoes

I've done a lot of thinking about, experimenting with, talking about, and eating of mashed potatoes. I have a few strong opinions. First and foremost, let's discuss the type of potato you will be mashing. Bakers, or russets, those beautiful, large, almost flawless football shaped potatoes, are not the potatoes for mashing; the smaller, lumpier, and more irregular shaped potatoes are. These have less water and more flavor and sugar than standard bakers. There are several specific varieties I like, such as Yellow Finnish and Yukon Golds, which mash marvelously into mashed potatoes of body and flavor. Potatoes have such a long life after harvest that they suffer the least of all vegetables from great cross-country trucking adventures. However, almost every part of the country has its own potato crops, and, as with all produce, fresher local potatoes will inevitably taste the best. Plus, you can feel good about supporting local trade.

So now you have selected your potatoes and it's time to cook them. Stop! Don't peel those potatoes! Rinse them, scrub them if you must, but please don't peel them. Potato skins hold in the flavor, nutrients, and texture while the potatoes boil. If you peel a potato before you boil it in water the water will taste like potatoes and the potatoes will taste like water. Fine for potato soup but hardly the thing for rich and yummy mashed potatoes. Also, season the cooking water well. If you don't salt the water, you'll be playing catch-up with the cooked potato and actually have to use more salt. Essentially, when salt is added at the cooking stage it enhances the flavor of food. Salt added afterwards never truly permeates the food and you will always taste the salt.

These are my three golden rules of mashed potatoes: use a thin-skinned, waxy potato, local if you can find them; cook them with the peel on; heavily season the water with salt and a little pepper if you choose. From this point, there really are no rules. I've mashed potatoes with sundried tomatoes, blue cheese, and even roasted jalapeños. In keeping with the nature of this treatise, the following recipe for mashed potatoes is pretty basic and basically delicious. Okay, my mother did raise an eyebrow at the garlic, but you've got to have a little room to explore.

GARLIC MASHED POTATOES

4   pounds thin-skinned, waxy
    potatoes
    Water to cover
1   tablespoon salt
5   cloves garlic, peeled
5   tablespoons butter
1/2 teaspoon or more black pep-
    per
1/2 cup buttermilk (approxi-
    mately)

SERVES 8.

Preparation

Clean the potatoes and place in a pot. Cover with water and add the salt and garlic cloves.

Bring to a boil and cook about 20 minutes until the potatoes are quite tender, but not falling apart. Drain the potatoes with the garlic. If you want to peel the potatoes, the skin will pull away very easily. Sometimes I like the added texture of the peel. Place the potatoes and garlic cloves, which will be very soft and mild in flavor now, in a large bowl and add the butter and pepper. Use a potato masher to smash 'em up, adding a little buttermilk to loosen them, but not so much as to make them sloppy. Taste for seasoning and adjust accordingly. Serve immediately or place in a casserole to reheat in the oven and get a crispy top.

POTATO AND PARSNIP PURÉE

You could also use turnips or salsify.

3   pounds thin-skinned, waxy
    potatoes
1   pound parsnips, peeled and
    cut in large chunks
1   tablespoon salt
1/2 teaspoon white pepper
1/2 cup butter
    Dash nutmeg
1/2 cup cream (approximately)

SERVES 8.

Preparation

Clean the potatoes and place in a pot with water 2 inches above the potatoes. Add the salt and pepper and bring to a boil. Add the parsnips and cook all until tender, about 15 minutes. Drain well and pull the skin from the potatoes. Place all in a food mill over a mixing bowl that holds the butter. Work the potatoes and parsnips through the food mill. Add the nutmeg to the potatoes and stir, incorporating the butter. Add the cream a little at a time until the desired consistency. Taste for seasoning and serve immediately.

SCALLOPED POTATOES

Be forewarned, this is a decadent and luscious dish.

SERVES 12.

Wash the potatoes and slice as thinly as possible with the skins on. Peel the onion and slice as thinly as possible. Layer the potatoes and onions in a casserole, sprinkling each layer with salt and pepper and a little cheese. Pour the cream over all and top with remaining cheese. Lightly sprinkle a little nutmeg on top. Cover with foil and bake at 350° until cooked through, testing with a knife, about 45 minutes. Remove the foil and brown the top. Serve hot.

This recipe makes a lot, but you will need a lot. I have never had any left over. In fact, I have discovered my guests in my kitchen after dinner, having at the crusty corners of the casserole with their fingers. This dish is rich and sinful and worth it.

COTTAGE FRIES

Growing up in the age of tater tots, homemade fries were a big treat for us. Even as a child, I could not get over how potato-ey they tasted compared to the frozen kind.

SERVES 6 TO 8.

Pour the oil in a deep cast iron skillet about two inches up. Heat the oil until very hot, but not smoking, about 325°. Fry the potatoes in batches, being careful not to overcrowd the pan. Drain the potatoes on paper bags placed over newspapers or a cardboard box. Salt and pepper and serve immediately.

POTATO PANCAKES

This is the way my mother always made potato pancakes, which we generally enjoyed for breakfast. We would pray for lots of leftover mashed potatoes on Saturday night so that we could wake up to these on Sunday.

SERVES 8.

2   pounds mashed potatoes (about 1 quart), chilled

½   cup all-purpose flour

3   tablespoons vegetable oil (or butter, or, what the heck, bacon fat)

Preparation

Form the mashed potatoes into eight ¼-pound patties. Lightly dust with flour. Heat half the fat in a skillet and and cook half the pancakes, turning once, until browned. They'll stay together better if you place them in the hot fat and leave them alone for a few minutes, forming a crust, before you attempt to turn them.

We usually had these with bacon and eggs, but they're great with grilled chicken, salmon, or pork tenderloin for dinner.

2   pounds small new potatoes

¼   cup olive oil

½   teaspoon salt

    Black pepper to taste

1   tablespoon fresh minced
     herbs

ROASTED NEW POTATOES

An easy and truly tasty side dish. Vary the herbs to match your mood.

SERVES 6.

Preparation

Preheat the oven to 400°. Use smaller potatoes, if possible. Clean and quarter the potatoes. Be sure they are fairly dry. Place in a bowl and pour the olive oil over. Add salt and pepper and toss the potatoes to coat evenly. Place on a baking sheet and roast in the oven until cooked through and nicely browned, about 20 minutes. You may need to turn the potatoes once during cooking. Remove from the oven and toss with the fresh herbs. I like to choose just one herb. Rosemary is traditional, and delicious with strong game. Parsley or basil are both nice, mint is unexpected and refreshing. Your choice.

These are quite tasty served hot or at room temperature, but I can not abide them straight from the fridge.

RICE

- 2 cups water
- 1 teaspoon salt
- 1 teaspoon butter
- 1 cup rice

Southerners have traditionally preferred a very fluffy white rice. In order to achieve this, rice is drained and well rinsed after it comes to a boil. This gets rid of most of the starch on the outside of the grains so that they don't stick together. Then you put the rice in a steamer and cook it very slowly. This is a simpler and starchier version.

One popular type of rice is an aromatic long-grain rice from Louisiana called popcorn rice. When it is cooking, the entire house will actually smell just like there's popcorn cooking. It tastes as good as it smells, too.

SERVES 4.

Preparation

Bring the water to a boil in a saucepan with the salt and butter. Stir in the rice and bring back to a boil. Stir once more, cover, and reduce the heat to very low. Cook for 15 minutes. Remove the lid and use a fork to fluff.

BAKED RICE

- 2 teaspoons butter
- 1/4 onion, minced
- 1 cup rice
- 2 cups well-seasoned chicken stock
- 1 bay leaf

So simple and so good. This will work with everything.

SERVES 8.

Preparation

Preheat the oven to 325°. Melt the butter in a saucepan and add the onion, cooking just to wilt. Stir in the rice, coating all the kernels with the butter, until the rice looks slightly opalescent. Stir in the stock and the bay leaf and bring to a boil. Reduce heat, stir and cover. Bake for 20 minutes, discard the bay leaf, and serve hot.

Ingredients

1 bunch salsify
  Juice of 1 lemon
3 tablespoons butter
1 tablespoon chopped parsley
1 teaspoon chopped chives

SALSIFY

Salsify is one of those vegetables which you think you might recall from an obscure Jane Austin novel. Actually, salsify was grown quite extensively here in the mid-South until the last few decades. Also referred to as Oyster Plant, salsify is a great starchy tuber and may be baked and mashed like a potato. This simple recipe adds a little herbal seasoning to a quick preparation.

Salsify is quite hairy and a bit frightening visually. Don't be alarmed. A paring knife will tame the beast.

SERVES 4.

Preparation

Wash and scrape the salsify. Place at once into cold water with the lemon juice. Bring a pot of salted water to a boil while cutting the salsify into 1-inch rounds. Cook the salsify in the boiling water until tender. Drain and return to the pan with the butter and additional salt and pepper to taste. Heat through, toss with the herbs, and serve.

Squash

Summer squash shares the same problem as most country and western music these days. There's too much of it and its basically bland and tasteless. However, just like Dwight Yoakim on a lonely night, there is yet some life and innocence in those pretty little yellow gourds. Little is definitely the key word here. The larger a summer squash, the woodier, starchier, and less flavorful. We must also remember that summer squash really is pretty fragile. Leave it alone in a brown paper bag inside your fridge for more than a day or two, and you will open that bag to find a lifeless and shriveled shell of a vegetable. Spare yourself and the squash the degradation. Buy small, very fresh yellow crookneck squash and cook it up that night.

Ingredients

- 2 **pounds yellow crookneck squash, cut in 1-inch thick circles**
- 1 **yellow onion, sliced**
- 1 **teaspoon salt**
- 1 **teaspoon black pepper**
- 1/4 **teaspoon cayenne pepper**
  Water
- 2 **tablespoons bacon grease**

COUNTRY SQUASH

Just the thing with fried chicken in the summer.

SERVES 6.

Preparation

Place the squash and onion with the salt and pepper in a heavy skillet and pour water about half way up. Bring to a boil. Stir, reduce the heat to medium, and cook until almost all of the water has evaporated. Add the bacon grease. Stir, reduce the heat to low, and continue to cook another 20 minutes, until the vegetables are cooked down and glossy.

STEAMED SUMMER SQUASH

Ingredients

- 2 pounds small, very fresh yellow crookneck squash
  Water
- ½ teaspoon salt
  Pinch white pepper
- 2 tablespoons butter
  Juice of 1 lemon
- 1 tablespoon roughly chopped fresh dill

Mama and Daddy have found a farmer at their market who brings in a variety of tiny little squash, crooknecks, zucchini, white patty pan, plus the golden round Sunburst. Mama combines these and lightly steams them on every possible night in the summer. They are truly beautiful, with a delicate, sweet flavor. We, my baby included, nibble on any leftovers cold the next day.

SERVES 6.

Preparation

Clean the squash well and trim the ends. Pour 1 inch of water into a pan fitted with a steamer. Bring the water to a boil. Place the squash in the top part of the steamer and sprinkle with salt and white pepper. Place inside the steam bath and turn the heat to medium. Cover and steam for 7 minutes.

Remove the squash to a saucepan. Add the remaining ingredients and toss to melt the butter and coat the squash with all. Serve warm.

PATTY PAN SQUASH WITH CHEESE GRITS

These are so pretty and delicious, I'd serve them with a little tomato sauce underneath as a first course at a fancy seated dinner. They're also a great addition to roasts or barbecues.

SERVES 6.

Ingredients

12	small patty pan squash
	Water
1	teaspoon salt
	Pinch white pepper
1	tablespoon olive oil (or butter)
1/2	yellow onion, diced
4	cloves garlic, minced
1	teaspoon tomato paste
3	cups water
1	cup grits
1/2	teaspoon salt
1/4	teaspoon black pepper
1	teaspoon minced fresh sage
1/2	cup grated sharp Cheddar cheese

Preparation

Bring the water to a boil with the salt. Add the squash and parboil about 2 minutes until just tender, depending on the size. Drain and cool. Scoop out about 1 tablespoon of squash from the body, using a spoon or melon baller.

Preheat the oven to 350°. Heat the olive oil in a saucepan and sauté the onion and garlic until translucent. Add the tomato paste and cook a couple of minutes, stirring. Pour in the water and bring to a boil. Stir in the grits and reduce the heat to medium. Cook for 20 minutes, stirring occasionally. Stir in the cheese and sage, and let cool slightly.

Spoon about 2 tablespoons of the grits into the hollow of the squash, mounding over the top. Place on a baking sheet and bake for 15 to 20 minutes, until heated through and slightly browned. These are nice on a picnic the following day.

2 pounds yellow squash (older,
    larger squash may be
    used here)
1 yellow onion, diced large
    Water
1 tablespoon salt
1 cup breadcrumbs (plus more
    for topping)
3 eggs
1 cup cream
2 tablespoons minced fresh
    basil
1 teaspoon black pepper
    Dash cayenne pepper
½ cup plus ½ cup grated sharp
    Cheddar cheese

SQUASH CASSEROLE

This is a great way to use up any larger or less than perfect squash with which you may be saddled. The casserole holds well and is good the next day. Really nice for a summer buffet.

SERVES 8.

Preparation

Preheat the oven to 350°. Clean the squash and cut in circles. Place in a pot along with the onion and cover with cold water. Add the salt and bring to a boil. Reduce the heat to medium and cook about 20 minutes until very tender. Drain well and place in a large mixing bowl. Add the breadcrumbs. Beat the eggs with the cream and mix into the squash. Stir in the fresh basil and ½ cup of grated cheese. Taste and add peppers and additional salt if needed. Pour into a baking dish and cover the top with additional breadcrumbs and the remaining ½ cup of grated cheese. Cover with aluminum foil. Bake at 350° for 30 minutes until the casserole is set.

Remove the foil and continue baking for 10 more minutes until browned on top.

4 sweet potatoes
¼ cup butter
    Salt and fresh ground black
    pepper to taste
    Dash ground cinnamon

BAKED SWEET POTATOES

Nature at its finest, merely heated up by man.

SERVES 8.

Preparation

Preheat the oven to 350°. Scrub the sweet potatoes clean and place right on the lower rack in the oven. Bake about 30 minutes until they are soft and squishy when squeezed. Cut the potatoes in half while they are still hot and stuff with butter. Sprinkle with salt, pepper, and cinnamon, and serve warm. I love these with lemon grilled chicken.

ROASTED SWEET POTATOES

So good I can eat a plate of them for dinner. A wonderful side for roast chicken in the fall.

SERVES 8.

- 4   sweet potatoes
- 1   red onion
- 2   tablespoons olive oil
    Salt and fresh ground black
      pepper to taste

Preparation

Preheat the oven to 400°. Scrub the potatoes clean and cut in quarters lengthwise. Cut these in halves. Likewise cut the peeled and cleaned red onion and place on a baking sheet. Pour the oil over and toss with salt and pepper. Roast in the oven about 20 minutes until tender and browned. Use a spatula to turn if needed to avoid burning. Lower the temperature, if necessary, to cook and brown the potatoes without burning. Serve hot or at room temperature. These are nice for a picnic, too.

FRIED SWEET POTATOES

The only way my Daddy will eat them.

SERVES 8.

- 4   sweet potatoes
    Vegetable oil
    Salt and pepper
    Pinch ground cinnamon, if
      desired

Preparation

Scrub the sweet potatoes clean and slice in thin circles. Heat 1-inch of vegetable oil in a heavy pan until the oil is wavy and glassy, about 325°. Fry the sweet potatoes, in batches if necessary, until nicely browned all over. Drain on clean paper bags, sprinkle with salt and pepper, and serve hot. If you use the cinnamon, mix it in with the salt before sprinkling over the potatoes.

Ingredients

4   sweet potatoes
1   Granny Smith apple, cored
    and sliced (I like to leave
    the peel on)
¼   cup butter
    Juice and zest of 1 orange
    Salt and white pepper to
        taste
    Pinch allspice

MASHED SWEET POTATOES

Smooth and satisfying. This is good living. Particular comforting when northern winds blow chilly and cold.

SERVES 6 TO 8.

Preparation

Bake the sweet potatoes as directed on page 94. Place the apples on a baking sheet and bake at the same time as the potatoes. The apples should cook for about 20 minutes, the potatoes for 30, until they are soft.

Remove from the oven and peel away the skins from the potatoes while they are still hot. They should pull away very easily (Use a dish towel if your fingers are sensitive.) Place the sweet potatoes in a bowl and lightly mash, leaving some lumps. Add the apples along with the remaining ingredients and stir together. Place in a baking dish and return to the oven to heat through and brown the top for about 20 minutes.

This is the definitive side dish for grilled or roasted pork tenderloin, or pork chops, fried or baked.

Tomatoes

Tomatoes are the vegetable that captures the very essence of summer. I hold them straight from the garden in my hands and feel the warmth that they hold and catch their perfume intensified by the sun. Should I eat you up right now, or slice you and give you a dollop of homemade mayonnaise? Should I stuff you or broil you, bake or sauté you, or just cut you in wedges and drizzle you with olive oil? Perhaps I'll just set you up in my windowsill and look at you for awhile.

2   ripe tomatoes
    Salt
2   tablespoons dried bread-
        crumbs
2   tablespoons Parmesan
        cheese
1   tablespoon minced fresh
        basil
    Freshly ground black pepper
        to taste

BROILED TOMATOES

A pretty, simple, and tasty vegetable. Really nice and fresh tasting with fish.

SERVES 6.

Preparation

Preheat the oven to broil. Wash the tomatoes and slice off the ends. Cut the tomato in 1½-inch slices and place on a broiling pan. Sprinkle with salt and a little breadcrumbs and cheese. Top with basil and black pepper. Broil about 7 minutes until the tomato is heated through and the topping is browned. Remove and serve immediately.

Great with steaks or grilled chilled chicken or fish. Even winter tomatoes are nice like this.

4 green tomatoes
½ cup cornmeal
1 tablespoon all-purpose flour
1 teaspoon salt
1 teaspoon black pepper
¼ teaspoon cayenne pepper (or
     to taste)
¼ cup vegetable oil

FRIED GREEN TOMATOES

Yes, they are for real. In fact, they are really good. We used to fry them on cookouts when I was a nine-year-old camper in the Cumberland Mountains. Come to think of it, those were the best I've ever had.

SERVES 6 TO 8.

Preparation

Slice the tomatoes ½-inch thick. Mix together the cornmeal, flour, salt, and black and cayenne pepper. Dredge the tomatoes in the coating on both sides and refrigerate for 30 minutes. This makes the coating stick.

Heat half the oil in a skillet and fry half of the tomatoes until browned on both sides, turning once, about 2 or 3 minutes per side. Drain on a clean paper bag and keep warm in a low oven.

Wipe out the skillet and heat the remaining oil. Fry the rest of the tomatoes, drain, and serve hot.

A classic breakfast with fried eggs and pork chops—great any time of the day.

TOMATOES STUFFED WITH HERBED RICE

This is a perfect light supper with a green salad or some cucumbers. Makes a nice side dish for a summer buffet.

SERVES 6.

- 6 homegrown tomatoes
- 1 tablespoon olive oil
- ½ yellow onion, diced fine
- 1 cup rice
- 2 cups flavorful chicken or vegetable stock
- 1 bay leaf
- 1 teaspoon salt
- 1 teaspoon white pepper
  Juice and zest of 1 lemon
- 1 tablespoon minced fresh parsley
- 1 tablespoon minced fresh basil
- 1 tablespoon minced fresh mint
- ½ cup fresh goat cheese, crumbled (plus extra for topping)

Preparation

Wash the tomatoes and slice off ½-inch at the tip end. Use a melon baller or small spoon to scoop out most of the pulp from the open tip end, being careful not to tear the sides. Reserve the pulp, discarding most of the seeds.

Heat the olive oil in a saucepan and stir in the onion. Cook until translucent. Stir in the rice and cook for a few minutes, until the kernels look pearly. Pour in the stock and stir, adding the bay leaf, salt and pepper. Bring to a boil. Stir, cover, and reduce the heat to low. Cover and cook for 15 minutes. Remove the lid and take off the heat. Discard the bay leaf and stir in the lemon juice and zest, herbs, and reserved tomato pulp. Allow to cool. Lightly stir in the crumbled cheese.

Preheat the oven to 350°. Stuff the tomato cavities full with the rice and top with a little additional cheese. Place the tomatoes core-side down on a baking sheet. Bake for about 20 minutes, until heated through and slightly browned on top.

Adding shrimp or crab meat to the rice makes a more substantial main course for a luncheon or light summer supper.

Ingredients

- 4 ripe tomatoes
- 2 ears corn
- 2 tablespoons olive oil
- 1 yellow onion, diced medium
- 1/2 bell pepper, diced medium
    (or 1 banana pepper,
    sliced in thin circles)
- 4 cloves garlic
- 2 teaspoons salt (or to taste)
    Fresh ground black pepper
- 1/2 cup red wine
    Juice of 1 lemon
- 1 tablespoon minced fresh
    basil
- 1 tablespoon minced fresh
    parsley
- 3 scallions, thinly sliced

TOMATOES WITH CORN

A yummy, mid-summer vegetable stew. Serve it over rice or with white bean croquettes for a meal in itself.

SERVES 6.

Preparation

Bring a large pot of water to a simmer. Fill a bowl with ice water. Rinse the tomatoes and cut out the core. Cut a slash in the tip end, and drop in the simmering water for about thirty seconds, until the skin pulls away easily. Use a slotted spoon to remove the tomatoes from the pot and drop into the ice water. Leave in the ice water until cool. Remove and drain in a colander. Pull away the skin and coarsely chop the tomatoes. Set aside in a bowl.

Shuck and clean the corn and cut the kernels from the cob. Set aside.

Heat the olive oil in a large skillet. Add the onion and cook until transparent. Add the pepper and garlic and cook, stirring occasionally, for 5 more minutes. Add the tomatoes along with the salt and pepper. Stir and cook for 5 minutes. Add the wine and lemon juice along with the corn. Stir, bring back to a simmer, and cook for 5 minutes. If the mixture is too runny, turn the heat to high and cook at a hard boil for a couple of minutes, being careful not to burn. Stir in the basil, parsley, and scallions, and serve immediately.

This could be a whole meal served over rice or pasta, or a great side dish for shrimp, fish, or chicken.

STEWED TOMATOES

Ingredients

- ¼ cup butter
- 2 yellow onions, diced
- 8 ripe tomatoes, peeled and coarsely chopped
- 1 tablespoon salt
- 1 tablespoon firmly packed brown sugar
- 2 tablespoons cider vinegar
   Dash cayenne pepper

Stewed tomatoes have been a conundrum to me. I love the idea, but for years and years every time I tried stewed tomatoes I almost spit them out. A case of too much sugar, and too little anything else. These stewed tomatoes finally work for me.

SERVES ABOUT 10.

Preparation

Heat the butter in a heavy saucepan, add the onions, and cook until translucent. Add all remaining ingredients, stir, and bring to a slow boil. Reduce the heat and cook uncovered, stirring frequently, for 30 minutes. The tomatoes should be thick and glossy.

4   medium turnips

2   tablespoons butter

Salt and white pepper to
    taste

Pinch nutmeg

1   teaspoon fresh parsley,
    minced

BOILED TURNIPS BROWNED IN BUTTER

Simple and lovely. A nice alternative to boiled new potatoes.

SERVES 6 TO 8.

Preparation

Peel the turnips and cut in large cubes. Place in a pot and cover with cold water. Add salt and bring to a boil. Reduce the heat to medium and cook about 10 minutes until tender but not mushy. Drain the turnips.

Heat the butter in a skillet and add the turnips, tossing to coat with the butter. Cook on medium about 7 minutes until browned, tossing occasionally. Sprinkle with salt, pepper, nutmeg, and parsley, and serve immediately.

These are nice with roast beef, turkey, or lamb. Flavorful and wholesome on a chilly evening.

Chapter 6

FRITTERS AND LITTLE

FRIED THINGS

*F*rying is a maligned, misunderstood, and mis-practiced craft. The idea that all fried foods are greasy comes from not knowing how to fry. Many years ago the fat that we used to fry in contributed to a greasy feel and flavor because animal fat, or lard, with all of its impurities cannot heat to a very high temperature before it smokes and burns. Food that is fried in lard usually absorbs a lot of fat, is not very pleasant to feel in the mouth, and to most of us is not very tasty. Certainly it is not easily digestible. However, polyunsaturated vegetable oils available to us today can heat to a much higher temperature (325° to 350°) before smoking. Something that is fried at the proper temperature actually develops a crispy crust that doesn't allow the fat to seep through. A higher temperature cooks more quickly, intensifying the natural flavor of the food (you don't want to cook at too high a temperature, though, or the outside will burn, leaving the center uncooked). Furthermore, some vegetable oils, particularly peanut oil, which Asians have used to fry and sauté with for centuries, are almost completely neutral in flavor, adding nothing which would detract from the taste of whatever you are frying.

Not to suggest that a fritter a day keeps the doctor away. Common sense tells us fried foods will never be health foods, but good ones at least will always be soul food.

Ingredients

2   cups corn kernels
1   tablespoon chopped parsley
1   tablespoon minced chives
1   teaspoon salt
1/2 teaspoon black pepper
1/4 cup all-purpose flour
1   teaspoon baking powder
2   beaten eggs
    Vegetable oil

CORN FRITTERS

These tasty little morsels can be served as a bread or side, or make a great first course served with a spicy mayonnaise or just hot sauce.

SERVES 4 TO 6.

Preparation

Stir all of the ingredients except the oil together in a mixing bowl. Let sit in the refrigerator for 1 hour. Pour 1 inch of vegetable oil in a heavy skillet and heat until you see waves cross the oil. Drop the fritters in the oil by spoonfuls and cook to brown on all sides. Drain on clean brown paper bags and sprinkle with salt before serving.

Ingredients

1   pound parsnips, peeled and
      cut in 1-inch pieces
2   teaspoons salt (plus
      additional, to taste)
1/2 teaspoons white pepper
    Dash grated nutmeg
1/2 cup all-purpose flour
2   eggs, beaten
    Vegetable oil

PARSNIP BALLS

These are great, a little pungent and spicy. Really good with roasted lamb or beef.

SERVES 6 TO 8.

Preparation

Place the parsnips in a pot and cover with water. Add the salt and bring to a boil. Cook about 10 minutes until the parsnips are tender. Drain, mash, and season with additional salt to taste, white pepper, and nutmeg. Add the flour and eggs, and chill about 1 hour until set. Pour 1 inch of vegetable oil in a heavy pot and heat to just under smoking, about 325°. Form the parsnip mixture into small balls and fry, turning to brown evenly.

Drain well and season with additional salt. I like to dip them in mustard.

1½ pounds lima beans (frozen may be used)

1 teaspoon salt (plus additional, to taste)

4 eggs

½ teaspoon white pepper

½ teaspoon minced fresh sage

½ cup cream

3 cups fresh grated bread-crumbs

Vegetable oil

LIMA BEAN CROQUETTES

I like to serve these with roast chicken and gravy.

SERVES 6.

Preparation

Rinse the lima beans, if fresh. Bring a pot of water to boil with 1 teaspoon salt and boil the limas about 15 minutes until tender. Drain, place in a bowl, and mash. It shouldn't be completely smooth; you will still have lumps. Mix with 2 eggs, salt if needed, pepper, sage, and cream. Refrigerate for at least 1 hour.

Pour 1 inch of vegetable oil in a heavy pot or deep skillet and heat to just below smoking, about 325°. Beat the remaining 2 eggs. Shape the lima beans into small balls. Dip in the egg and then in the breadcrumbs. Fry until golden brown, turning, and drain on clean brown paper bags. Season with salt and serve.

WHITE BEAN CROQUETTES

Wonderful as a side for any meal. I like to serve them with tomato sauce and a green salad as a complete meal.

SERVES 6 TO 8.

- ½ pound dry white beans
- 2 teaspoons salt (plus additional, to taste)
- ¼ teaspoon cayenne pepper
- 2 tablespoons butter
- 2 eggs
- 1 tablespoon chopped green onion
   Paprika
- 2 cups crushed cracker crumbs
   Vegetable oil

Preparation

Place the beans in a pot with the salt and cover with water. Bring to a boil. Turn off the heat and let sit in the water for 1 hour. Drain, rinse, and place the beans back in the pot with 1 teaspoon salt, the cayenne, and water to cover. Bring to a boil and cook about 1 hour until very tender.

Beat 1 of the eggs. Drain the beans, mash slightly, and stir in the butter, 1 beaten egg, green onion, and paprika. Chill and form into balls.

Beat the remaining egg. Dip the balls in the egg, roll in the cracker crumbs, and chill again for 30 minutes.

Pour 1 inch of vegetable oil in a heavy pot or skillet. Heat to just under smoking, about 325°. Fry the croquettes until golden brown, turning to brown evenly. Drain on clean brown paper bags, sprinkle with salt, and serve with hot sauce or Tomato Sauce (see recipe, page 113).

2   cups plain boiled rice
3   eggs
1/4 onion, grated
1   teaspoon lemon juice
1/2 teaspoon salt
1/4 teaspoon black pepper
1   tablespoon chopped parsley
2   tablespoons milk or cream
1/2 cup all-purpose flour
3   cups dry breadcrumbs
    Vegetable oil

RICE CROQUETTES

A perfect use for leftover rice. Great as an appetizer, or with any roasted meat. Try breaking them open and ladling stew or hash over.

SERVES 4 TO 6.

Preparation

Mix the rice with 1 beaten egg, the onion, lemon juice, salt, pepper, parsley, and cream. Refrigerate for 30 minutes. Place the flour, 2 beaten eggs, and breadcrumbs in separate shallow dishes. Shape the rice mixture into balls. Roll lightly in the flour, dip in the egg, and roll in the breadcrumbs. Refrigerate for 30 more minutes.

Pour 1 inch of vegetable oil in a heavy pot or skillet. Heat to just under smoking, about 325°. Fry the croquettes until golden brown, turning to brown evenly. Drain on clean brown paper bags, season with salt, and serve.

3   sweet potatoes
1   tablespoon butter
1   egg yolk
    Salt to taste
    Cayenne and white pepper to
      taste
    Dash ground cinnamon
1/2 cup chopped pecans
1   egg, beaten
2   cups dry breadcrumbs
    Vegetable oil

SWEET POTATO CROQUETTES

A great sweet but savory accompaniment for turkey or pork.

SERVES 6.

Preparation

Preheat the oven to 350°. Rinse the sweet potatoes and bake for 30 minutes, until soft. Peel and mash while still hot, along with the butter and 1 egg yolk. Mix in the seasoning and nuts. Chill for 30 minutes. Form into balls, dip in the beaten egg, and roll in the breadcrumbs. Refrigerate while the oil is heating. Pour 1 inch of vegetable oil in a heavy pot or skillet. Heat to just under smoking, about 325°. Fry the croquettes until golden brown, turning to brown evenly. Drain on clean brown paper bags, sprinkle with salt, and serve.

HUSH PUPPIES

The mandatory accompaniment to any fish fry—any good one, that is.

SERVES 4 TO 6.

Ingredients

- 2 cups white cornmeal
- 1 teaspoon baking powder
- 1 onion, finely chopped
- 2 stalks celery, finely chopped
- 1 cup buttermilk
- 1/4 cup shortening, melted
- 1/2 teaspoon salt
- 1/4 teaspoon black pepper
- 1/4 teaspoon paprika
- 2 eggs
  Vegetable oil

Preparation

Mix together everything but the oil. Refrigerate while the oil is heating. Pour 3 inches of vegetable oil in a deep skillet, or use a deep fat fryer. Drop the batter by tablespoonfuls into the hot oil and fry until golden brown. Drain on clean brown paper bags, sprinkle with salt, and serve hot with fried catfish, trout, shrimp, or oysters.

Chapter 7

SEAFOOD

As you may have guessed, this will be a short chapter. This is not on account of my temperament. On the contrary, I would eat sea creatures with every meal, if they were fresh and briny as the ocean itself. That is the problem. Tennessee, for all of its many virtues, has one thing lacking: an ocean.

Now we do have catfish and trout in abundance, and these we celebrate with gusto, cornmeal, and lots of hot sauce. As to salt water creatures, oysters and shrimp are the delicacies that traditionally have made the long inland trek to pots and pans in Nashville. Nowadays, anything is possible with fish being air freighted. But before anything was possible, lots of good things were around.

Ingredients

1 quart oysters
  Salt and black pepper to
    taste
  Cayenne pepper to taste
½ cup butter
  Juice of 1 lemon
1 quart soda cracker crumbs
1 scant cup cream

SCALLOPED OYSTERS

It took me the longest time to figure out why there have always been oysters in cookbooks and on bills of fare in land-locked Tennessee from the early eighteen hundreds on. Then I discovered that oysters were actually shipped live on ice and fed cornmeal throughout their journey. One more good reason to traditionally eat oysters in the colder months.

Scalloped oysters are standard fare at many Thanksgiving dinners in the South. Rich and oh, so tasty, these are really quite simple to prepare.

SERVES 12.

Preparation

Preheat the oven to 400°. Place a layer of oysters in the bottom of a baking dish. Sprinkle with a little salt, pepper, and cayenne. Dot with butter, sprinkle with lemon juice, and layer cracker crumbs over. Arrange one or two more layers, ending in cracker crumbs. Pour the cream over just to moisten. Bake uncovered for 15 to 20 minutes and serve.

4 *slices bacon*

1 *onion, chopped*

4 *cloves garlic, minced*

2 *ribs celery, chopped*

1 *carrot, peeled and cut in ½-inch circles*

1 *teaspoon minced fresh thyme leaves*

1 *teaspoon minced fresh rosemary leaves*

2 *tablespoons all-purpose flour*

4 *cups milk*

1 *pint oysters with liquid*

OYSTER STEW

This is an excellent winter meal. Simple and satisfying.

SERVES 6.

Preparation

Cook the bacon and reserve. Pour the fat into a large saucepan and cook the onion for about 5 minutes, until wilted. Add the garlic, celery, carrot, thyme, and rosemary, and cook another 5 minutes. Stir in the flour and brown slightly. Stir in the milk and bring to a slight boil. Reduce to a simmer and cook for 15 minutes. Stir in the oysters and about half of the liquid, strained. Heat to just under boiling and cook until the oysters are slightly curled. Serve at once with rice or corn bread. Crumble bacon on top, if desired.

Be careful reheating this. The oysters can become chewy if boiled and the liquid may break. Best to serve immediately.

Ingredients

24 large oysters
 1 teaspoon salt
¼ teaspoon black pepper
¼ teaspoon cayenne pepper
 2 eggs
 1 tablespoon water
 3 cups toasted breadcrumbs
    Oil for deep-frying

DEEP-FRIED OYSTERS

These make the best Po Boy Sandwich. But I usually just squeeze some lemon on them and pop them in my mouth.

SERVES 4 TO 6.

Preparation

Pick through the oysters. Drain well and pat dry. Sprinkle with salt and peppers. Beat the eggs with the water in a shallow bowl. Place the bread crumbs on a plate. Roll each oyster in the breadcrumbs, then the egg, and again in the breadcrumbs. Refrigerate for 30 minutes. Heat the oil in a deep fat fryer to 325°. Fry the oysters for about 1½ minutes, until golden brown. Drain on clean brown paper bags. Serve with Hush Puppies (see recipe, page 108), and Tartar Sauce (recipe follows).

Ingredients

 1 cup mayonnaise
 1 tablespoon sweet relish
    Juice of 1 lemon
    Dash cayenne pepper

TARTAR SAUCE

MAKES ABOUT 1 CUP.

Preparation

Combine all of the ingredients in a medium bowl and mix well.

DEEP-FRIED FROGS' LEGS

Frogs' legs are a traditional food throughout the South. Commercially packed frogs' legs, large and meaty, can be purchased frozen. And yes, they do taste quite a bit like chicken.

SERVES 2 TO 4.

Ingredients

6   pair frogs' legs
    Boiling water
    Salt and pepper to taste
2   eggs, beaten
1   cup dry breadcrumbs
    Oil for deep-frying

Preparation

Wash the frogs legs. Boil water and pour over. Let sit for 5 minutes. Drain and dry. Sprinkle with salt and pepper. Dip in the egg and dredge in the crumbs. Heat the oil in a deep fat fryer to 325°. Fry the frogs' legs for about 5 minutes. Drain on clean brown paper bags, sprinkle with salt, and serve with Tomato Sauce (recipe follows).

TOMATO SAUCE

MAKES ABOUT 4 CUPS.

Ingredients

2   tablespoons olive oil
1   large onion, finely chopped
1   red bell pepper, seeded and
      finely chopped
6   cloves garlic, minced
2   tablespoons tomato paste
1   28-ounce can tomatoes
½   cup red wine
2   teaspoons salt
1   teaspoon sugar
1   teaspoon dried oregano
1   teaspoon dried thyme
1   teaspoon dried basil
1   bay leaf

Preparation

Heat the olive oil in a deep skillet or broad saucepan and add the onion. Cook on high for 5 minutes. Add the bell pepper and garlic and cook 5 more minutes, stirring occasionally to prevent burning the garlic, which gets very bitter if it burns. Stir in the tomato paste and cook a couple of minutes. Add the tomatoes, squeezing them with your hand to break them up and pouring in the juice from the tomatoes and the wine. Add the remaining ingredients, stir, and bring the mixture to a boil. Turn the heat to medium low and cook, stirring occasionally, for 1 hour.

Adjust the seasoning. Discard the bay leaf. This will be good for several days.

Ingredients

- 3 pounds shrimp
- 1 gallon water
- 2 lemons, halved
- 2 green onions, rough chopped
- 3 sprigs parsley
- 1 celery stalk, roughly chopped
- 1 bay leaf
- 1 teaspoon salt
- 1 teaspoon cayenne pepper

BOILED SHRIMP

Shrimp boiled in the shell will always give much more flavor than those that are first peeled. Besides, getting a little messy is part of the fun with eating a plate of boiled shrimp.

I was taught the craft of boiling shrimp by one of my best friends, Steve Scalise, the executive chef at The Corner Market in Nashville, who just happens to be from New Orleans. Like everything Steve cooks, it's more of a method than a recipe. Improvisation is an important part of Steve's life in general. And in life in general and boiling shrimp in particular, the seasonings can change. Just follow the time and the how-to's. Steve's never failed me, and this won't fail you.

SERVES ABOUT 4 FOR A MAIN COURSE.

Preparation

Rinse the shrimp and set aside, keeping them cool. Pour the water in a large pot with the the rest of the ingredients. Bring to rolling boil and cook for 5 minutes. Throw in the shrimp, bring back to a boil, and cook about 4 minutes. Don't overcook! You can see that the shrimp are cooked when the flesh pulls slightly away from the shell. Pull the pot off the heat and toss in a good sized bowl of ice. This will stop the cooking without rinsing away the flavors. If the ice melts very quickly, add some more. Let the shrimp steep in the liquid for 5 minutes, then drain and chill the shrimp in the fridge. Serve with Cocktail Sauce (recipe follows), lots of lemon, and plenty of paper towels.

COCKTAIL SAUCE

Ingredients

2   cups catsup
1/4 cup prepared horseradish
     Juice of 1 lemon
1   teaspoon hot sauce
2   cloves garlic, minced
1/4 onion, grated

Preparation

Mix together and serve with shrimp and oysters, boiled and fried.

DEEP-FRIED SHRIMP

Ingredients

     Oil for deep-frying
3   pounds large shrimp
1   cup all-purpose flour
1   cup cornmeal
1/2 teaspoon garlic powder
1/2 teaspoon salt
1/2 teaspoon black pepper
1   tablespoon hot sauce

Nashville is an eight-hour drive from the closest beach, the Redneck Riviera, or as most of the world knows it, the Florida Panhandle. All jesting aside, these beaches are beautiful white sand, until recently quite pristine. My parents became engaged down there, and as a family we spent a week there every year. While we were vacationing, we always gorged ourselves on as much shrimp as we could possibly consume and packed coolers with more to bring home. Deep-fried shrimp is a feast of celebration, especially dear to us in this land-locked state.

SERVES 4 TO 6.

Preparation

Heat the oil in a deep fryer to 325°. Peel and clean the shrimp, leaving the tail on. Mix the flour and meal with the seasonings on a plate. Pour the hot sauce on the shrimp and toss. Dredge the shrimp in the flour mixture and deep fry for about 3 minutes. Drain on clean brown paper bags, sprinkle with salt, and serve with lemon and Cocktail Sauce (recipe precedes) or Tartar Sauce (see recipe, page 112).

FRIED BROOK TROUT

Beautiful trout grace the streams throughout the mid-South. This makes a very tasty breakfast for hungry fishermen just home with their catch. Thankfully, fresh trout is available at just about every seafood counter, so you can have this for breakfast, lunch, or dinner, fishermen friends or no.

SERVES 4.

Ingredients

- 4 fresh brook trout, cleaned
  Salt and pepper to taste
  Dash paprika
- ½ cup all-purpose flour
- 1 egg
- 1 cup dry breadcrumbs
  Vegetable oil

Preparation

Rinse the fish and pat dry. Sprinkle with the salt, pepper, and paprika. Heat ½ inch of vegetable oil in a heavy skillet. Lightly run the fish through the flour, dip in the egg, and then dredge in the crumbs. Place cut-side down in the hot oil and fry for 1½ minutes. Turn and fry for 1½ minutes more. Drain well and serve with lots of lemon.

1   cup flaked salmon
2   medium potatoes
½   teaspoon salt
¼   teaspoon black pepper
1   teaspoon lemon juice
1   tablespoon fresh chopped
      parsley
2   teaspoons sliced green
      onions
1   egg
      Oil for deep-frying

SALMON BALLS

These probably became popular in the mid-South because you could make them with canned salmon, the only kind available until very recently. You could, of course, cook fresh salmon, but a quality canned brand works fine for these.

SERVES 4.

Preparation

Pick through the salmon and refrigerate until ready to use. Cook the cleaned potatoes with skins on in salted water as for mashed potatoes until easily pierced with a fork. Peel and mash. Beat 1 cup of the mashed potatoes with the salmon and other ingredients except the oil. Refrigerate for 30 minutes.

While the salmon mixture is cooling, heat the oil in a deep fat fryer to 325°. Form the mixture into balls and fry until golden brown. Drain on clean brown paper bags, sprinkle with salt, and serve with lemon.

6   nice-sized catfish fillets
1½ cups buttermilk
½   cup all-purpose flour
½   cup cornmeal
    Salt and pepper to taste
    Vegetable oil
2   lemons, cut in wedges

FRIED CATFISH

The stuff that dreams are made of. Catfish is so creamy and light. You can prepare it a number of perhaps more healthful ways, but this is by far its most common form and a true taste sensation and flavor delight.

SERVES 6.

Preparation

Rinse the catfish. Pour the buttermilk in a shallow bowl and set the fish in this in the refrigerator for 1 hour. Mix the flour and meal with the salt and pepper. Pour ½ inch of oil in a heavy skillet and heat to just under smoking. Lift the fish from the milk and dredge in the flour mixture. Place inside-side down in the oil and fry for about 4 minutes per side. Drain and serve with lemon.

Chapter 8
POLULTRY

The South is not alone in its love affair with poultry. Particularly in these low-fat days, I feel that poultry is frequently lauded as the perfect protein. I myself am re-romanced by free range chicken, that is, chicken as our grandparents knew it on the farm. Chicken with a little color to its meat, not bleached pure white by chemicals, hormones, and synthetic feed. Chicken that has a taste of poultry, not cardboard. Obviously, free range chicken is more expensive, prohibiting most of us from eating it three or four nights a week. But maybe if more and more of us sample this higher quality chicken and are introduced to what chicken or poultry can really taste like, maybe then more of us will demand it and more suppliers will supply it. That, my friends, is how the price comes down. Democracy and a free market in action. Glory be.

FRIED CHICKEN

4   pounds cut-up chicken
    pieces, your choice
1½ cups buttermilk
1   cup self-rising flour
1   teaspoon salt
1   teaspoon black pepper
¼   teaspoon cayenne pepper
½   teaspoon garlic powder
1   teaspoon paprika
1   egg
    Vegetable oil

Where would we be without fried chicken? What would we have eaten at all of those picnics and Sunday dinners? Would our accents be different? Would we walk with a quicker gate? Luckily these are frightening questions which we need not ponder, for there has always been and will always be fried chicken in the South.

After contemplating the many methods of frying chicken with all of their nuances, advantages, and disadvantages, I settled on one method which, quite frankly, makes a damn good fried chicken.

ABOUT 8 SERVINGS.

Preparation

Rinse the chicken pieces and soak in 1 cup buttermilk in the refrigerator for at least 2 hours or overnight.

Stir together the flour and seasonings and place on a plate. Beat the egg together with the remaining buttermilk. Heat oil about 1 inch deep in a skillet.

Remove the chicken from the buttermilk and dredge in the flour. Dip in the egg mixture, then dredge again in the flour. Fry until cooked through, about 15 to 20 minutes. Drain on clean brown paper bags and season with salt.

CHICKEN GRAVY

Some people seem frightened of gravy, but, I promise you, there is no great mystery here. If you do get some little lumps, just pour it through a strainer.

Preparation

Pour all but 3 tablespoons of the fat from the frying pan, leaving the crumbs left from the chicken. Add 3 tablespoons of all-purpose flour, and cook, stirring constantly, until lightly browned, but not burnt, or it will be hopelessly bitter. Slowly add 2½ cups of good chicken stock. Stir and cook slowly about 20 minutes until the gravy is browned and thickened. Season with salt and pepper, and serve separately from the chicken.

A lot of people use milk instead of water.

FRIED LIVERS AND GIZZARDS

People get really funny about just what innards they will and will not eat. I myself am a born liver lover, but I would not deign to nibble on a gizzard. I've been told it goes both ways. Some gizzard people hate the texture of livers. Luckily, especially if both camps dwell in your home, they both are cooked the same way for about the same amount of time.

Preparation

Prepare just as you would for fried chicken, but cut the cooking time down to 5 to 7 minutes. Serve with gravy.

CHICKEN AND DUMPLINGS

This smells and tastes like somebody loves you.

SERVES 8.

- 3 pounds chicken pieces
- 1 onion, chopped
- 3 stalks celery, chopped
- 2 carrots, peeled and chopped
- 1 bell pepper, chopped
- 3 cloves garlic, minced
- 2 bay leaves
- 1 teaspoon dried thyme leaves
- 4 sprigs parsley
- 2 teaspoons salt
- ½ teaspoon black pepper
  Dash cayenne pepper

Preparation

Rinse the chicken and place in a Dutch oven with the remaining ingredients. Cover with cold water and bring to a slight boil. Reduce the heat to low, cover, and simmer until tender, about 1 hour or more. Remove the chicken pieces and, when cool enough to handle, skin and bone them, leaving the meat in large chunks. Leave the meat out of the pot as you prepare the dumplings (recipe follows).

BISCUIT DUMPLINGS

SERVES 8.

Ingredients

- 1 cup all-purpose flour
- 2 teaspoons baking powder
- ½ teaspoon salt
- ½ cup milk

Preparation

Skim as much fat as possible from the top of the broth. Heat the broth to a slow steady boil. Mix together the flour, baking powder, and salt. Stir in the milk and beat until stiff. Drop by spoonfuls into the boiling broth. Cover and cook for 10 minutes Add the meat back in and cook 5 more minutes. The dumplings should be puffed and the meat warmed through. Serve hot.

- 4 skin-on bone-in chicken breasts
- ¼ cup olive oil or butter
- ½ onion, chopped
- 3 cloves garlic, minced
- 3 ribs celery, chopped
- 2 cups rice
- 1 pint mushrooms, cut in quarters
- 4 cups good chicken broth
  Juice of 1 lemon
- 1 teaspoon dried thyme
- 1 bay leaf
- 2 teaspoons salt
- ½ teaspoon black pepper

CHICKEN BAKED IN RICE

This makes for a wonderfully robust dinner. I like to serve chicken and rice with something a little sweet, like fried apples, and maybe a simple spinach salad.

SERVES 4.

Preparation

Preheat the oven to 375°. Rinse the chicken breasts and pat dry. Season with salt and pepper. Heat the oil or butter in a heavy ovenproof saucepan wide enough to hold the breasts. Place the breasts skin-side down in the pan and sprinkle the onion around the breasts. When the onion begins to soften, add the garlic and celery. Turn the chicken to brown both sides. When both sides are lightly browned and the vegetables are wilted, stir in the rice to coat with fat. Stir in the mushrooms, stock, lemon juice, and the seasonings, and bring to a light boil. Stir and cover. Bake for 20 minutes until the rice is done and all of the stock is absorbed.

This makes a lot of rice, but it is so delicious, you'll be happy to have some left over, if indeed you do.

CHICKEN POT PIE

Ingredients

- 1 whole chicken
  Cold water to cover
- 2 onions
- 3 ribs celery
- 2 bay leaves
- 4 sprigs fresh thyme (or 1 teaspoon dried)
- 4 or 5 sprigs parsley
- 1 tablespoon salt
- 1 teaspoon white pepper
- 1/2 teaspoon cayenne pepper

- 1/4 cup butter
- 1 onion, chopped
- 2 ribs celery, chopped
- 2 carrots, peeled and cut in 1/2-inch pieces
- 2 parsnips, peeled and cut in 1/2-inch pieces
- 1/2 pound mushrooms, cut in quarters
- 1/4 cup frozen small peas
- 1/4 cup all-purpose flour
- 2 cups chicken broth (or more)
- 1 teaspoon fresh thyme leaves
- 1 tablespoon chopped parsley
- 1 scallion, cut in thin circles

This is one of the first main courses that I really started to play with as a budding young cook. You can put any combination of complementary vegetables in here. Sometimes I use sweet potato or winter squash for a little sweetness. Try lima beans or corn. Mama makes a great chicken pie with pork sausage, too. The possibilities are endless.

You can also use any form of cooked chicken you may have, but this method supplies you with a rich broth, as well. You should have enough left over to make some soup.

SERVES 6.

Preparation

Rinse the chicken well and remove the giblets. You may cook the neck with the chicken, but not the other stuff. Place the chicken in a large pot and cover with cold water. Add the 2 onions, 3 ribs of celery, bay leaves, sprigs of fresh thyme, sprigs of parsley, salt, pepper, and cayenne, and bring to a boil. Skim off any scum and turn the pot down to a simmer. Simmer for about 40 minutes.

Remove the chicken and let cool. Strain the broth and, if you like, you can simmer the broth, reducing it and getting a more concentrated flavor. Reduce, if you wish, for about 30 minutes.

Meanwhile, remove the skin from the chicken and pull the meat from the bones. Cool until ready to use.

Melt the butter in a large skillet and sauté the chopped onion until wilted. Add the chopped celery, carrots, parsnips, mushrooms, and peas, and cook for about 10 minutes. Reduce the heat, stir in the flour, and cook, stirring constantly, for about 5 minutes, letting the flour brown slightly. Slowly pour in the broth, stirring constantly. The sauce will thicken. Let the thickened sauce cook slowly for about 10 minutes, adding more stock if the sauce is too thick. . Stir in the chicken and fresh herbs and adjust the seasoning. Remove from the heat and pour all into a baking dish.

Preheat the oven to 400°. Make up one recipe of Buttermilk Biscuit dough (see recipe, page 160). Roll out 1/2-inch thickness and cut to cover the top of the baking dish. Place the cut out dough over the filling. Cut slits in the dough and brush with melted butter. Bake for about 10 to 15 minutes until the pastry is puffed and brown.

CHICKEN PIQUANT FOR BARBECUE

This has a subtle, tangy flavor that I love. You can bake it fully in the oven if a grill isn't convenient, but you won't get the same flavor.

SERVES 6.

Ingredients

- 1/2 onion, grated
- 3 cloves garlic, minced
- 1 teaspoon salt
- 1/4 cup chopped parsley
- 1 teaspoon dry mustard
- 1/4 teaspoon black pepper
- 1 teaspoon Worcestershire sauce
- 1 tablespoon Louisiana-style hot sauce
- 2 tablespoons vegetable oil
- 6 large pieces bone-in skin-on chicken, leg or breast quarters

Preparation

Combine all of the ingredients except the chicken and place in a baking dish. Rinse the chicken and let marinate in the baking dish for at least 1 and up to 12 hours. The chicken will get spicier the longer it marinates.

Preheat the oven to 375°. Cover the chicken in the marinade with aluminum foil and bake for 30 minutes. Remove the chicken from the marinade and broil on a medium hot grill until cooked through with a crispy skin.

Serve with Potato Salad (see recipe, page 34), Cole Slaw (see recipe, page 35), and a couple of other things, too.

1   roasting chicken
1   onion, quartered
1   bay leaf
3   cloves garlic, mashed
2   tablespoons butter, some-
       what softened
       Juice of 1 lemon
1   teaspoon salt
¼   teaspoon black pepper
¼   teaspoon cayenne pepper
1   teaspoon fresh thyme leaves

ROAST CHICKEN

Hard to resist when it's really done well. Leftovers make the best sandwiches.

SERVES 2 TO 4.

Preparation

Preheat the oven to 400°. Remove the giblets and rinse the chicken inside and out. Pat dry. Sprinkle some salt and pepper inside the body and stuff in the onion and bay leaf. Truss the chicken very simply by tying the legs together at the bottom joint and tying the wings up close to the body. There are a zillion ways to do this. Do what works for you. The idea behind trussing is not to make a perfect football shape for beauty's sake, but to get all of the parts held up close to the body in order to insure even cooking time. Trussing should not be a stressful experience.

Mash the garlic through a press or in a mortar and pestle with the salt sprinkled over. Mix with the butter, lemon, and the rest of the seasonings. Rub this paste all over the chicken, particularly getting up under the skin and rubbing on the meat itself. Place the chicken breast-side down on a rack inside a roasting pan and place in the oven at 400°. After 10 minutes, turn the oven down to 350°. Jiggle the chicken a bit to keep the breasts from sticking to the rack. Roast for 30 minutes.

Turn the chicken over to brown the breasts. Roast for at least 10 more minutes breast-side up, until a thermometer inserted in the thick of the thigh joint registers at least 160°. Let the chicken rest for 10 minutes before carving.

You may use the drippings from the bottom of the pan to make a gravy. Pour them into a saucepan and heat. Stir in about 3 tablespoons of flour and cook until the flour browns slightly. Stir in 2 cups of good chicken stock, stirring constantly. Bring to a boil and turn down to a simmer. Season with salt and lots of pepper and let cook for 20 minutes. Serve in a gravy boat.

CREAMED CHICKEN

Yummy, smooth and as comforting as a favorite blanket.

SERVES 6.

4 chicken breasts
1 onion, halved
1 stalk celery
2 teaspoons salt
1/2 teaspoon white pepper
1 bay leaf

1/4 cup butter
1/2 onion, minced
1/4 cup all-purpose flour
2 cups milk
1/4 teaspoon salt
   White pepper to taste
   Dash nutmeg

Preparation

Rinse the breasts and place in a pot. Cover with cold water, add 1 onion and the seasonings, and bring to a boil. Reduce the heat to a simmer and cook about 15 minutes until tender. Remove the chicken and let cool. Strain the broth and return to the stove on low heat. Let the broth reduce on low while you finish preparing the chicken.

Melt the butter in a saucepan. Add the onion and cook until wilted. Stir in the flour. Cook about 5 minutes, stirring constantly. Slowly add the milk, stirring or whisking out any lumps. If you still have lumps, don't fret. You can strain the sauce later. Cook the sauce for 20 minutes. The sauce should not have any flour taste left to it. Add the chicken and thin the sauce out some with about 1/2 cup of the reduced broth. Taste and season accordingly (your broth could be pretty salty by now). Let the chicken heat through and serve over steamed rice, popovers, or cornmeal waffles.

CHICKEN CROQUETTES

Mother is the great chicken croquette maker in our family. We tend to have these frequently for birthday parties, but they are one thing the entire extended family really loves.

I've also made smaller croquettes for large buffets. Nice because they're tasty at room temperature as well as hot.

SERVES 6.

Preparation

Cook and pull chicken as you did for creamed chicken (see recipe, page 127) and prepare the white sauce, leaving out the extra broth. Cut the chicken meat into small pieces and place the chicken in a bowl along with the juice of 1 lemon, half of an onion, finely minced, and 1 rib of celery, finely minced. Pour just enough white sauce in to bind the chicken; it should not be too saucy. Taste for seasoning. You may need additional salt and pepper. Let the mixture cool for an hour or so to firm up. Grate 4 cups of fresh breadcrumbs and beat 2 eggs. Form the chicken into balls a little larger than golf balls. Roll in the breadcrumbs, dip in the egg, and then roll in the breadcrumbs again, pressing the crumbs in.

Refrigerate the croquettes while you heat vegetable oil in a deep fat fryer. When the oil has reached 325°, fry the croquettes a few at a time, draining them on box tops lined with clean brown paper bags. Makes about 18 small croquettes, to serve six. Serve

BRUNSWICK STEW

Oh my, people do get stewed up about just what goes into a Brunswick Stew. Originally, I believe that a lot of squirrel found its way into the pot, and maybe a little pork as well. It varies from pot to pot. I've limited the pork to bacon drippings and cut the squirrel out altogether, but if you happen to have a freezer full of squirrel, by all means, throw it in. Rabbit really does work well also. Burgoo is a very similar stew that is served in Kentucky. Lima beans are requisite in Burgoo. Stews, I believe, are open to interpretation and some artistic license. If it tastes good, most folks don't care what you call it.

SERVES 10.

Ingredients

- 1 whole chicken
- 2 onions, halved
- 3 ribs celery, roughly chopped
- 2 carrots, roughly chopped
-    Water to cover
- 2 bay leaves
- 4 sprigs fresh thyme (or 1 teaspoon dried)
- 4 sprigs parsley
- 2 teaspoons salt
- 1 teaspoon white pepper
- 1/4 teaspoon cayenne pepper
-    Fat from frying 4 slices bacon
- 1 large onion, chopped
- 6 cloves garlic, minced
- 1 bell pepper, chopped
- 1 cup sliced okra
- 1 28-ounce can tomatoes
- 1 tablespoon red wine vinegar
- 2 cups chicken broth (or more)
-    Kernels from 2 ears corn
- 1 1/2 cups fresh butter beans
- 3 small potatoes, cut in 1-inch pieces
- 2 teaspoons salt
- 1 teaspoon black pepper
- 1/4 teaspoon cayenne pepper
- 1 bay leaf
- 1 teaspoon thyme leaves
- 1 teaspoon dried basil
- 2 teaspoons Worcestershire sauce

Preparation

Rinse the chicken and remove the giblets. Place in a pot with the onions, celery, and carrots, and cover with cold water. Bring to a boil along with the seasoning. Reduce the heat to simmer and cook about 40 minutes until tender. Remove the chicken and let cool. Strain the stock and set aside.

Remove the skin from the chicken and pull the meat from the bones. Cool until ready to use.

Fry the bacon in a Dutch oven. Remove the bacon and cook the onion in bacon fat for about 3 minutes. Add the garlic, pepper, and okra, and cook on high heat about 5 minutes. Add the tomatoes and vinegar and cook on high about 10 minutes. Add the stock and bring to a boil. Reduce the heat to medium and add the remaining ingredients. Add more stock if necessary, and adjust the seasoning. Cook until the vegetables are very tender and the liquid is slightly thickened.

Stir in the chicken and heat through. Taste again for seasoning and serve in bowls over rice.

1   16-pound turkey
1/2 cup butter, softened
1   tablespoon salt
1   tablespoon black pepper
1   teaspoon cayenne pepper

ROAST TURKEY WITH CORN BREAD STUFFING

The quintessential Thanksgiving dinner is very hard to beat. It tastes just as good at other times of the year as well.

SERVES 16.

Preparation

Preheat the oven to 400°. Remove the giblets from the turkey and rinse. Pat dry. Mix together the butter with the salt and peppers. Rub this inside and outside of the turkey, pushing up under the skin to season the meat. Loosely fill the bird with corn bread stuffing and tie the legs together at the bottom joint. Place breast-side down on a rack fitted inside of a roasting pan and roast for 1 hour. Baste the bird well with the pan juices and turn down to 350°. Roast for about 3 hours, basting every 20 minutes, and then turn the bird over, breast-side up. Continue roasting until the middle of the stuffing registers 160°. Remove from the oven and let the bird sit for at least 20 minutes before carving. Serve with Giblet Gravy (see recipe, page 132) and cranberry sauce.

1 loaf corn light bread, broken
   up in rough cubes (see
   recipe, page 154)
1 loaf white bread, broken or
   torn in rough cubes
4 slices bacon
1 large onion, finely chopped
6 cloves garlic, minced
3 stalks celery, finely chopped
2 carrots, finely chopped
   About 4 cups good chicken
   stock
1 tablespoon fresh sage,
   minced (or 2 teaspoons
   dried crushed)
1 tablespoon chopped parsley
2 scallions, thinly sliced
   Salt and pepper to taste

CORN BREAD STUFFING

SERVES 16.

Preparation

Place the bread pieces in a large mixing bowl. Set aside. Cook the bacon in a large skillet. Remove the cooked bacon and reserve for another use. Briefly cook the onions, garlic, celery, and carrots in the bacon drippings, just to wilt them. Add to the mixing bowl along with the drippings. Heat the chicken stock to a good boil and pour two thirds of it into the stuffing, along with the remaining ingredients. Mix well and taste. Adjust the seasoning and the consistency with additional stock, as needed. Remember that cooking the stuffing in the bird will moisten it somewhat.

THANKSGIVING NIGHT TURKEY SANDWICH

Preparation

I feel a little silly giving a recipe for this, but I can't stop talking about turkey until I cover this important topic. Our big Thanksgiving dinner occurs at approximately one o'clock in the afternoon. And, needless to say, it is BIG. But when six o'clock rolls around, something in our bellies cry out from habit for attention. This is what we give our bellies. A roast turkey sandwich. Executed on white bread with mayonnaise, preferably homemade, and garlic salt. That's it. Perfection.

GIBLET GRAVY

Ingredients

3   cups chicken broth from
      cooking the chicken
1   tablespoon butter
1/2 onion, minced
1   rib celery, minced
      Giblets from the chicken, cut
      in small pieces
      Meat pulled from neck bone
1   hard-boiled egg, chopped
      small
1   teaspoon cornstarch
      Salt and pepper to taste
1   tablespoon chopped
      parsley
1   tablespoon chopped
      scallions

ABOUT 1 QUART.

Preparation

Heat the broth in a saucepan to a slow boil and keep warm. Melt the butter in another saucepan to sizzling and cook the onion and celery for 2 or 3 minutes. Add the giblets and neck meat and cook for 3 more minutes. Pour in the broth and bring back to boil. Taste for salt and pepper and adjust the seasoning. Add the egg and let the gravy cook slowly for 20 minutes. Mix the cornstarch with 1 tablespoon of water and stir into the gravy. Bring to a boil. The gravy should thicken slightly. Remove from the heat, stir in the parsley and scallions, and serve.

TURKEY HASH

Ingredients

1/4 cup butter
1   onion, chopped
3   ribs celery, chopped
1/4 cup all-purpose flour
4   cups chicken stock
8   small new potatoes, quar-
      tered
      Salt and pepper to taste
      Dash Worcestershire sauce
4   cups pulled turkey meat

Usually served the Friday after Thanksgiving dinner, but so good you really shouldn't wait for just once a year. You can also make this with chicken.

SERVES 8 TO 10.

Preparation

Melt the butter and cook the onion and celery until wilted. Stir in the flour and cook until slightly browned. Stir in the stock and bring to a boil, stirring. Add the new potatoes and turn the heat down to medium. Taste and add salt and pepper. Cook for 20 minutes. Add the turkey meat and cook another 10 minutes. Serve over corn or batter cakes.

ROAST QUAIL WITH BACON

8 quail
   Salt and black pepper to
     taste
1 teaspoon minced fresh thyme
8 slices bacon
1 tablespoon bourbon
2 cups chicken stock

Quail are very plentiful in our woods, and now they're easy to find commercially, so you don't have to rely on a hunter friend. Quail are so small, they really should be cooked quickly or they dry out.

SERVES 4.

Preparation

P reheat the oven to 425°. Rinse the quail and pat dry. Season inside and out with salt and pepper (easy on the salt, remember the bacon is mighty salty). Sprinkle thyme leaves over the outside. Wrap one piece of bacon around each quail, making a neat little bundle. Place the birds on a rack fitted into a shallow roasting pan. Roast the birds for about 15 minutes. Remove from the oven and remove the rack with the quail from the roasting pan. Set the roasting pan on top of the stove. Splash in the bourbon, being careful of any flames (it will only flame if directly ignited with flame from a gas burner). Pour in the stock, bring to a boil and reduce until slightly thickened. Serve the quail with mashed potatoes and the sauce over both.

Note: Dove may be cooked the same way. They are especially good prepared this way and cooked on a medium grill.

Ingredients

2 rabbits
¼ cup cider vinegar
   Salt and black pepper to
      taste
3 tablespoons dry mustard
2 tablespoons all-purpose
      flour
4 slices bacon
1 onion, chopped
4 cloves garlic, minced
3 cups chicken stock
2 bay leaves

PAN-BAKED RABBIT

*I realize that rabbits do not have wings, but they taste and cook so
similarly to chicken that this is the chapter I chose to include them.*

*Rabbit is a wonderful meat, tasty, healthful, and plentiful.
Better for the environment than some forms of livestock, in that they
don't take up much space or require a lot of feed in proportion to the
meat that they produce.*

*This is a great hunter-style recipe with a lot of character and
heartiness. I like it best in the cold weather months.*

SERVES 8.

Preparation

Preheat the oven to 300°. Rinse the rabbits and cut into serving
pieces (quarters). Pour the vinegar over and work into the meat.
Mix together the salt and pepper, mustard, and flour, and rub all
over the rabbit. Cook the bacon in a large Dutch oven and
remove when cooked. Add the rabbit and brown evenly on all
sides. Add the onion and garlic to the pot about half way through
browning the rabbit. Pour in the chicken stock and add the bay
leaves. Bring the stock to a boil and cover the pot. Bake for about
1 hour. Remove the top. Continue cooking for 30 minutes. The
meat should be very tender and the stock reduced to a nice sauce.
This is great with buttered or mashed turnips or scalloped
parsnips.

Chapter 9

MEATS

❧

While bowls of vegetables, salads, and relishes fill the canvas of a southern table, the meat platter is the energy source around which they revolve. Today, most of us are removed from the agricultural life by only one or two generations. Our grandparents or great grandparents rose with the sun and labored most of the day. They ate as heartily as they worked, and the livestock they fed was the livestock which in turn fed them. Beef, pork, and lamb are all mainstays of our culinary heritage, originally raised and slaughtered responsibly on small farms where children were made aware of the cycle of life and death at an early age. Today, so many of the meats available to us are pumped with hormones and chemicals and slaughtered under circumstances of questionable sanitation. Happily, as the public is made ever more aware, we continue to demand safer and more humane treatment of livestock, in life and death. While the immediate result may raise meat prices, the end results are worth it: immensely tastier meat which is more healthful and a more sound manner in which to treat the earth. After all, we are all God's stewards.

Beef

Beef has traditionally been used more for dairy than for butchering in these parts. Remember that the South has never been a really wealthy area except for a very few for a very short while. Cuts of beef tend not to be choice and are frequently extended into stews or meat loaves. These not so choice cuts, however, are usually loaded with flavor. You just have to work on them a bit more.

CHICKEN-FRIED STEAK

Ingredients

2	pounds round steak, cut into 6 thin pieces
1	cup all-purpose flour
½	teaspoon salt
¼	teaspoon black pepper
1	egg, beaten
¼	cup butter
3	tablespoons fat
3	tablespoons all purpose flour
2	cups water
	Salt and pepper to taste

I asked my mother if she ever ate steak like this as a child, and she responded that this was the only way she ever ate steak. Times change pretty quickly. There is no chicken involved in this recipe, but the beef steak is battered and fried as one would a piece of chicken. Maybe not a nutritionally sound notion for every night of the week, but very beneficial for the soul now and then, especially on a cold, dark night.

SERVES 6.

Preparation

Sprinkle a little salt on the steaks and use a mallet to pound the steaks well. Season 1 cup of flour with the ½ teaspoon of salt and ¼ teaspoon pepper and dredge the steaks in this. Dip them in the beaten egg and dredge again in the seasoned flour. Heat the butter in a heavy skillet. Add the steaks and cook over medium high heat about 1½ minutes per side, longer for thicker cuts. Don't overcook or they'll get tough. Remove the steaks from the pan and keep warm while you make gravy.

You should have some fat left in the pan after you remove the steaks. If you don't, add a little more butter so that you have about 3 tablespoons of fat in the pan. Stir in 3 tablespoons of flour and cook, stirring, until it browns. Pour in the water, stirring, and bring to a boil. Reduce the heat and cook about 5 or 10 minutes. Season with salt and pepper and serve with the steaks. Mashed potatoes are a natural with this meal.

FRIED CALF'S LIVER

You love it or you hate. I love it, especially like this. Calf's liver is prepared in the same fashion as the steaks.

SERVES 6.

Rinse the liver and soak in the buttermilk for an hour. Mix the salt and pepper with the flour and set on plate. Cook the bacon in a heavy skillet and remove when done. Dredge the liver in the flour. Dip in the beaten egg and dredge in the flour again. Cook the liver in the bacon fat for 4 minutes per side. Serve with Glazed Onions (see recipe, page 76) and crumble the bacon on top.

Ingredients

- 6   slices calf's liver
- 1   cup buttermilk
- 1/2   teaspoon salt
- 1/4   teaspoon black pepper
- 1   cup all-purpose flour
- 6   strips bacon
- 2   eggs

POT ROAST

I like my pot roast falling apart with lots of yummy vegetables and some good gravy in the pot. This will deliver.

SERVES ABOUT 12.

Preheat the oven to 300°. Cook the bacon in a Dutch oven or skillet and remove when done, leaving the drippings. Mix the flour with the seasonings on a plate. Rinse the roast and dredge in the flour. Brown the roast in the bacon grease. Pour in the stock. If the stock is not very flavorful, you should add a little salt and pepper to taste. Cover the roast and bake for 3 hours, until the roast is exquisitely tender. Add the vegetables, coating them with the pan juices. If most of the stock has cooked out, add a little more, or about 1/2 cup of red wine. Cook uncovered for 1 more hour.

Ingredients

- 3   slices bacon
- 5   pounds chuck roast
- 2   cups all-purpose flour
- 1   teaspoon salt
- 1/2   teaspoon black pepper
- 1/2   teaspoon dried thyme
- 1   quart beef stock
- 6   onions, peeled and quartered
- 8   potatoes, cut in large cubes
- 12   carrots, peeled and cut in large pieces
- 1/2   cup red wine (optional)
     Additional stock

Ingredients

2 pounds ground chuck

1 pound pork sausage

1 onion, chopped

6 cloves garlic, minced

2 ribs celery, chopped

1 red bell pepper, chopped

1½ teaspoons salt

½ teaspoon black pepper

¼ teaspoon cayenne pepper

1 teaspoon dried oregano

1 teaspoon dried sage

⅔ cup tomato purée

⅓ cup Dijon mustard

2 teaspoons Worcestershire sauce

1 egg

½ cup breadcrumbs

MEAT LOAF

Meat loaf can be as wonderful as the maker. Put some love into it, and your meat loaf, your friends, and your family will all love you back.

SERVES 8 TO 10.

Preparation

Use a large mixing bowl to mix everything together. If you use your hands, it's a good idea to wear rubber gloves. Form into 2 rounds or pack into loaf pans. Bake at 400° for about 1 hour until completely cooked through.

Serve with Brown Gravy (recipe follows).

Ingredients

3 tablespoons butter

3 tablespoons all-purpose flour

2 cups rich beef stock

Dash soy sauce

Salt and pepper to taste

BROWN GRAVY FOR MEAT LOAF

Use a good canned or frozen stock.

Preparation

Heat the butter in a saucepan and stir in the flour. Cook, stirring constantly, until lightly browned. Stir in the stock, bring to a boil, and simmer for 15 minutes. Add soy sauce, salt, and pepper.

MEAT PIE

You can make this up in an instant with leftover stew, and everyone will think you have done something really special. You have, of course, but with a casual nonchalance that lends an attractive air of mystery to your person. In other words, folks will be amazed.

This savory pie is yummy and satisfying with any juicy, slow-cooked meat such as pot roast or beef brisket. I like to make pies from stew, because I like all of the vegetables.

SERVES 8.

Ingredients

6   cups beef stew
1   recipe pie dough (see recipe, page 195)
1   egg mixed with 2 table-spoons milk

Preparation

Preheat the oven to 375°. If the stew is very thick, just spoon about 6 cups of it into a baking dish. If the stew is a little runny, use a slotted spoon to leave some of the juice behind.

Roll out the pastry and cut a little wider than the baking dish. Cover the stew and crimp the edges. If you have some dough left over, you can use that to cut out leaves, hearts, or other designs to top your pie. Stir the egg and milk together and use a pastry brush to paint it over the pastry. If you are using any cut-outs, place them on top of the painted dough and paint these, as well. Make a few slits in the pastry and bake for 20 to 30 minutes, until the pastry is browned and the stew is bubbly.

Ingredients

1   cup all-purpose flour

1   teaspoon salt

1/2 teaspoon black pepper

4   pounds beef chuck, cut into
      10-inch cubes

3   tablespoons vegetable oil

1   tablespoon tomato paste

3   cups beef stock

1   teaspoon dried thyme

1   teaspoon dried oregano

1   bay leaf

1/2 cup red wine
      Additional salt and pepper
      to taste

3   tablespoons butter

1   large onion, chopped

6   cloves garlic, minced

2   carrots, cut in 1-inch pieces

6   new potatoes, quartered

2   medium turnips, peeled and
      cut in 1-inch pieces

1   pint mushrooms, quartered
      Salt and pepper to taste

BEEF STEW

Hearty and hale, beef stew takes the edge off the cold and smooths out the bumps of the day. This gets better the second day.

SERVES ABOUT 12.

Preparation

Mix the flour, salt, and pepper together on a plate. Dredge the cubed beef in the flour. Heat the vegetable oil in a Dutch oven and brown the meat on all sides. Stir in the tomato paste and cook for a couple of minutes. Pour in the stock, herbs, and wine. Taste the liquid and add salt and pepper if necessary. Bring to a boil, stir, and reduce the heat to low. Cover and cook for 1 hour and 30 minutes. Heat the butter in a large skillet and sauté the onion, garlic, and carrots for about 5 minutes. Remove the cover from the stew and stir in the sautéed vegetables along with the potatoes and turnips. Add more stock, if necessary, to cover all of the vegetables. Cook for 30 minutes, then stir in the mushrooms. Adjust the seasoning and cook for 30 minutes more. Serve in bowls or over corn cakes.

SPICED ROUND

In an odd culinary digression for Nashville, German meat-packers set up shop in town in the mid-eighteen hundreds and introduced the mid-South to Spiced Round, a round of beef that is generously larded throughout with strips of spiced pork fat, and then aged in brine. The meat is purchased after brining to be cooked at home, as you would a corned beef. Nashville's spiced rounds have been rather famous —especially around holiday times —for generations, although you don't see them as frequently now as when my parents were young.

My immediate family didn't often cook spiced rounds. We didn't have to because Aunt Sue always did. I remember them at her house for Christmas and New Year's. She purchased one with a lot of mustard in the pork fat, creating perfect yellow circles in a pale pink roast. Quite exotic if not frightening to a small child, yet I, of course, had to eat it, to the dismay of sisters and cousins alike. Seeing that much glorified fat is a bit odd to modern American minds, but it is, truly, delicious. The roast itself is so lean and briny that the fat rather balances it. What can I say. You simply have to try it.

Here's how to cook a spiced round once you get it home.

Preparation

Soak the spiced round in cold water for 1 hour. Remove the round from the water. Place on a rack in the bottom of a very large pot. Wrap the roast a couple of times around with heavy foil to preserve the tightly formed shape. Place the round on the rack and cover with cold water. Stir in 1 cup of brown sugar. Bring to a boil, reduce to a simmer, and cook for 15 minutes per pound. Remove and let cool. Rewrap in more foil and chill in the refrigerator. Slice thinly and serve cold with mustard if desired.

Ingredients

1   leg of lamb, about 5 pounds
½ cup butter
6   cloves garlic, cut in slivers
1   teaspoon salt
½ teaspoon black pepper
    Leaves from 2 sprigs fresh
     rosemary
10 new potatoes, scrubbed and
     cut in halves

ROAST LAMB

Roast lamb can be really horrible: stringy, gray, and dry. That said, this lamb is juicy and flavorful, with a crispy outside and and a little pink inside. The potatoes are divine.

SERVES ABOUT 8.

Preparation

Preheat oven to 400°. Make a paste of the butter and seasonings, and rub all over the lamb. Place in a roasting pan and cook for 15 minutes. Turn the oven down to 350° and cook the lamb for 1 hour. Stir the potatoes into the pan juices and cook at least 30 more minutes, until the potatoes are cooked through and the lamb is cooked to your desire, about 145° for medium. Remove the lamb from the pan and keep the potatoes warm. Let the lamb sit outside of the oven for at least 10 minutes before you slice it. If you don't, all of the juices will spill out and onto your cutting board. Slice the meat and place on a platter with the potatoes around. Pour any pan juices over the lamb and serve.

It is most traditional to serve roast lamb with a mint jelly of which, I have to tell you, I am not too fond. I prefer to serve roast lamb with Southern Fried Apples (recipe follows) or a nice chutney. If you miss the mint flavor, try stirring some roughly chopped mint into the apples.

10 tart young apples, unpeeled,
       sliced
3/4 cup firmly packed brown
       sugar
1/4 cup butter (or 3 tablespoons
       butter and 1 tablespoon
       bacon fat)
1 cup water
1/2 teaspoon ground cinnamon

SOUTHERN FRIED APPLES

These go with a thousand things, every meat you imagine.

SERVES ABOUT 8.

Preparation

Place everything together in a heavy skillet and stir until the sugar dissolves. Cover and cook over low heat for 20 minutes. Remove the cover and cook 5 or 10 more minutes until the liquid is almost all cooked out. Serve warm.

Pork

Southerners probably eat more pork than anyone else in the country. When I went to culinary school in New York, I sometimes felt like pork was considered a lower class of meat. This, of course, is absurd. Pork has enormous flavor, cooks beautifully, and can be one of the healthiest meats you could eat, depending on the cut. Pork popularity is definitely on the upswing, however. Pork has proudly found its way onto the menu of many a swank restaurant, and its virtues are being extolled by nutritionists, economists, and environmentalists alike. Let's hear it for pork.

SLOW-BAKED PORK CHOPS

A great meal for company. It gives you almost an hour to relax and will hold in a warm oven well after that.

SERVES 8.

Ingredients

8   thick pork chops

1   cup all-purpose flour

1   teaspoon salt

1/2   teaspoon black pepper

3   tablespoons butter

2   tart apples, cored and cut in thick slices

2   onions, cut in thick slices

1   cup chicken stock

1   teaspoon minced fresh thyme leaves

Preparation

Preheat the oven to 325°. Rinse the pork chops and pat dry. Mix the flour, salt, and pepper together on a plate. Heat the butter in a Dutch oven or deep skillet and brown the pork chops about 4 minutes per side. Stir in the apples and onions and cook about 3 minutes. Stir in the stock and thyme. Cover and bake for 45 minutes to an hour, checking occasionally to make sure the stock has not cooked out, until the pork is very tender.

Heaven with mashed potatoes.

PAN-FRIED PORK CHOPS

Tasty, tasty!

SERVES 4.

8 thin-sliced pork chops, 2 per person

1/2 cup all-purpose flour

1/2 teaspoon salt

1/2 teaspoon black pepper

3 tablespoons butter

Preparation

Rinse the pork chops and pat dry. Mix the flour, salt, and pepper together on a plate and dredge the chops in this. Heat the butter in a skillet and fry the chops about 5 minutes per side. If you'd like a gravy, make as with Chicken Fried Steak, (see recipe, page 136). A strong vinegary pickle is also good, such as chow chow or green tomato pickle or corn relish.

Mama usually serves applesauce with these.

BARBECUED PORK SHOULDER

A great meal for a summer party and really fool-proofed by doing most of the cooking prior to the grilling.

SERVES 6 TO 8.

Ingredients

1   3- to 4-pound pork shoulder
    Water to cover
1   tablespoon salt
1   tablespoon black pepper
3   cayenne peppers

2   teaspoons salt
2   teaspoons black pepper
2   cloves garlic, minced
1   teaspoon cayenne pepper
¼   cup vegetable oil

Preparation

Have the butcher butterfly the pork shoulder. Rinse it and place in a large pot. Cover with water and add the salt and peppers. Bring to a slow boil and cook for 1 hour.

Have the grill lit and cooking at a medium heat. Remove the pork from the water and pat dry.

Combine all of the remaining ingredients and rub into the meat. Place the meat over medium-low coals, off-center from the strongest heat, and cook about 30 minutes, turning now and then. Most people like for at least part of outside to get quite crispy. My sisters and I always fought over the crispy pieces.

Remove from the grill and let sit for about 10 minutes before slicing and serving with your choice of barbecue sauce. Following are two I like.

VINEGAR BARBECUE SAUCE

2 tablespoons oil
3/4 cup white vinegar
2 tablespoons Worcestershire sauce
1 tablespoon firmly packed brown sugar
1/2 onion, grated
Juice of 1 lemon
1 teaspoon cayenne pepper (or more)

MAKES ABOUT 3 CUPS.

Preparation

Mix everything together and let sit for at least 1 hour, or—even better—overnight.

RED BARBECUE SAUCE

1/4 cup vegetable oil
1/2 onion, coarsely grated
6 cloves garlic, minced
2 fresh cayenne peppers, minced
1 cup ketchup
3/4 cup vinegar
1/4 teaspoon ground cinnamon
1/2 teaspoon celery seed
1/2 teaspoon black pepper

MAKES ABOUT 3 CUPS.

Preparation

Heat the vegetable oil in a heavy saucepan and add the onion, garlic, and cayenne. Cook, stirring, for 5 minutes. Add the remaining ingredients and bring to a boil, stirring occasionally. Taste for seasoning. Simmer for 10 minutes, then let cool.

Country Ham

Country ham is a peculiarly Southern delicacy, beloved here for literally centuries, which only recently is gaining much acceptance outside of the South. Salted, smoked, and aged country ham is very intensely flavored, truly nothing like a fresh or lightly smoked ham that one might thickly slice and take large bites of. Country ham is generally nibbled, stuffed into biscuits, and the scraps used to flavor beans, greens, soups, and stews. A country ham lasts awhile.

Daddy used to receive one for Christmas and hang it out in his work room until spring. I remember a Yankee chum whose folks had just moved here from Ohio looking wide-eyed at the very large and slightly moldy hind quarter of pork dangling from a beam by a rope. I, of course, had never given it much thought.

Over the years I grew quite weary of people saying that country ham was too salty and too fatty and, oh, how could I eat that. Recently I've almost grown tired of seeing it over-used on fashionable menus.

I honestly believe that country ham owes something of its new-found acceptance to the vast and recent popularity of prosciutto, country ham's almost equally salty and, oh, so trendy Italian cousin. Hey, Italians eat grits, too, don't they? Hmm.

TO COOK A COUNTRY HAM

Preparation

Use a wire brush to scrub the outside of a ham. Soak the ham overnight. Fill a very large pot about two-thirds full of water and bring to a boil. Place the ham in the pot, return to a rapid boil, and reduce the heat to get a slow, steady boil. Cook for 30 minutes per pound of meat. Remove the meat and let cool, reserving as much of the cooking liquid as you have room for in your fridge or freezer for cooking beans and soups.

GLAZED COUNTRY HAM

1   country ham, cooked as
      described on page 148
1   cup prepared mustard
1   cup firmly packed brown
      sugar

SERVES UP TO 20.

Preparation

Preheat the oven to 350°. Remove the outer skin and score the fat in a diamond pattern. Press in several cloves at cross points in the scoring. Spread the mustard on the ham and press in the brown sugar. Bake just long enough to heat the ham through and caramelize the glaze, about 30 minutes.

COUNTRY HAM STEAKS WITH RED EYE GRAVY

4   country ham steaks
1   cup water

We usually had these for dinner on Sunday night when I was growing up. A whole steak is pretty salty to eat by itself (my father would argue this point). I usually stuff a piece of ham steak in my biscuit and add a dab of butter.

SERVES 4.

Preparation

Leave a white rim of fat around the steaks. If the fat has a tough outer coating, score it to keep it from pulling the meat while it cooks. Heat the skillet to medium and cook the steaks for about 3 minutes per side. Remove the steaks and keep warm. Leave any fat in the pan and heat to smoking. Pour the water into the pan, scraping up any little browned bits on the bottom. Heat to just under boiling. Serve in a sauce boat along with the ham. Most people like to pour it over their biscuits.

Ingredients

4 pounds ground pork
6 cloves garlic, minced
1 tablespoon salt
1 tablespoon red pepper flakes
1½ teaspoons black pepper
1½ tablespoons fresh sage,
   minced

BREAKFAST SAUSAGE

This is really easy to make and very, very tasty. How nice to know exactly what's in it as well!

MAKES ABOUT 20 BREAKFAST-SIZE PATTIES.

Preparation

Place all ingredients in a bowl and mix together very thoroughly. Shape into patties and cook in a skillet over medium heat until browned and cooked through.

If this recipe makes more than you will use in one meal, you may shape your patties, wrap, and freeze them. Use within one month to avoid freezer burn.

Ingredients

1 pound bulk sausage meat
2 tablespoons all-purpose
   flour
4 cups milk, heated

SAUSAGE GRAVY

A real luxury which I rarely allow myself. This will serve as breakfast and lunch in one.

SERVES 6.

Preparation

Brown the sausage meat in a skillet on medium high, crumbling the sausage as it cooks. Remove the meat, reduce the heat to medium low, and stir in the flour, scraping browned bits up from the pan. Stir and cook for 3 minutes. Pour in the warm milk, stirring out any lumps. Raise the heat and cook on medium, stirring occasionally, for 15 minutes. Add the sausage back to the pan and heat through. Serve over warm, split buttermilk biscuits.

Chapter 10

BREADS

❧

$\mathcal{I}$ love to cook all different types of bread, bringing plates of biscuits and muffins, or pans of corn bread to the table. So many of us have grown accustomed to packaged breads and rolls. While they do serve to mop up the juices on your plate, they can't possibly compete with the satisfaction of freshly made breads. Packaged breads can't give your home the sweet, warm smell of fresh rolls or corn bread in the oven, and none of them could possibly give the flavor of scratch-made goods. Waffles in the toaster, pancakes in the microwave, biscuits from a can, I guess they all have their place in this absurdly busy society that we have managed to create for ourselves, but a few nights, maybe just one night a week or one night a month, do yourself a favor and take twenty minutes to make up some biscuits or mix up some corn bread. And if you really have some time, try a batch of yeast rolls or honey whole wheat bread. You can't imagine the magic that happens with a package of yeast, some dry goods, and a pair of hands. It's more than chemistry.

Ingredients

1   cup coarse white cornmeal
½   teaspoon salt
½   cup water
1   tablespoon butter, melted
¼   teaspoon baking soda
½   cup buttermilk

CORN PONES

The South's romance with cornmeal is centuries old and still going strong. I always try to use stone-ground meal from a small mill. The sweet flavor of corn almost mystically shines when a good meal is cooked. There are probably a hundred types of corn bread flavored with vegetables, herbs, and cheese. Corn breads may be baked or fried. A pone is kind of in between the two.

Pones are cooked on a hot greased griddle in the oven. This lets them rise and gives them a crispy outside.

MAKES ABOUT 10 SMALL PONES.

Preparation

Preheat the oven to 450°. Mix the meal with the salt in a medium bowl. Bring the water to a boil and pour into the meal mixture. Add the melted butter. Dissolve the soda in the buttermilk and add to the meal. Form into balls and flatten out on a hot greased griddle. Bake in the oven until browned on one side. Turn and brown on the other.

Serve hot with butter and sorghum for breakfast, or with greens or fried fish.

2 cups good cornmeal
½ teaspoon salt
2 cups boiling water
   Vegetable oil

HOT WATER CORN BREAD

These are so good. They're even better if you use a quality stone ground cornmeal from a small mill. This is a fine example of sublime simplicity.

MAKES ABOUT 12 SMALL PIECES OF CORN BREAD.

Preparation

Stir the cornmeal and salt together in a large bowl. Heat about ½-inch of oil in a skillet. Pour the hot water over the meal and stir together to a thick mash. Drop by spoonfuls into the hot oil and fry until golden brown all over. Drain on a clean brown paper bag and sprinkle with more salt.

4 sweet potatoes
1 egg
2 cups stone-ground cornmeal
1 teaspoon salt
½ teaspoon baking soda
1 tablespoon shortening, melted
½ cup buttermilk (about)

SWEET POTATO PONES

The rich sweet potatoes and cornmeal really complement each other. Try heating any leftovers for breakfast with honey or sorghum.

MAKES ABOUT 16 PONES.

Preparation

Preheat the oven to 350°. Bake the sweet potatoes in their skins for about 45 minutes until very soft. Peel and mash while still hot. Beat in the egg, then stir in everything but the buttermilk. Add just enough buttermilk to make a stiff batter. Form into small balls and flatten slightly onto a hot greased griddle. Bake for about 30 minutes. Serve hot with butter. Try these with fresh pork.

Ingredients

2 cups stone-ground cornmeal

1/4 cup sugar

1/2 teaspoon salt

1 teaspoon baking soda

1 cup buttermilk

2 tablespoons shortening

CORN LIGHT BREAD

This is another one of Mama's recipes, but I have cut way back on the sugar which I think makes it a more well rounded bread. The texture of this is like a dense bread, perfect for slicing. It makes a great corn bread stuffing and is divine with barbecued pork shoulder.

SERVES 6 TO 8.

Preparation

Preheat the oven to 350°. Grease and flour a medium loaf pan. Mix the dry ingredients together in a mixing bowl. Stir in the buttermilk. Melt the shortening and add, mixing well. Pour into the prepared loaf pan and bake about 40 minutes, until cooked through and browned .

Ingredients

1 1/2 cups water

1 1/2 tablespoons shortening, melted

1 cup cornmeal

3 whole eggs, well beaten

1 cup milk

1 tablespoon baking powder

1/4 teaspoon salt

SPOON BREAD

So good. Passing the spoon bread around the table just seems to bring a family closer together.

SERVES 8.

Preparation

Heat the water with the shortening in a saucepan. Bring to a boil and pour over the meal in a medium bowl. Stir until blended and cool. Stir in the eggs, milk, salt, and baking powder. Mix thoroughly and pour into a well greased 8-inch baking dish or cake pan. Bake for 30 minutes until firm. Serve in the baking dish with butter.

BUTTERMILK CORN BREAD

A classic recipe. Very fast and simple. You'll wonder why you don't make it more often.

SERVES 8 TO 10.

- 2   cups cornmeal
- 1   teaspoon salt
- 1   teaspoon baking soda
- 2   cups buttermilk
- 2   eggs
- 1   tablespoon bacon fat or
      butter

Preparation

Preheat the oven to 375°. Mix the dry ingredients in a large bowl. Pour in the buttermilk and beat in the eggs. Melt the fat in a cast-iron skillet. Pour in the batter and bake in the skillet for 20 to 25 minutes, until risen and browned.

FRESH CORN BATTER CAKES

Ella Hayes (Miss Ella to me) fried these for the whole family and all of their guests in their house on Monteagle Mountain straight through her eighty-seventh year. She would cook the bacon first and use the drippings for cooking the corn cakes. That could get anyone out of bed.

MAKES ABOUT 10 CAKES.

- 2   to 4 ears sweet corn
- 2   cups all-purpose flour
- 1   teaspoon baking powder
- 1   teaspoon salt
- 1   tablespoon butter
- 1   cup milk
- 1   egg

Preparation

If the corn seems really tough, you can boil it a few minutes first. With good, sweet corn there's no need. Scrape the corn from the cob to get 1 cup. Sift together the flour, baking powder, and salt. Melt the butter and stir in along with the milk. Beat the egg and mix in. Stir in the grated corn. Cook on a lightly greased griddle on top of the stove, turning once. Serve hot.

Ingredients

1   cup water
2   cups coarse cornmeal
1   teaspoon salt
1   cup cracklings
1/4   teaspoon baking soda
3/4   cup buttermilk

CRACKLING PONES

Cracklings are made from pork skin and give this bread an unforgettable rich flavor. They're still sold in a lot of neighborhood grocery stores, or ask your butcher about them.

MAKES ABOUT 16 PONES.

Preparation

Preheat the oven to 425°. Boil the water and pour over the cornmeal in a large bowl. Stir. Add the salt and cracklings. Dissolve the soda in the buttermilk and stir into the mixture, mixing thoroughly. Form balls and flatten onto a hot greased griddle. Bake until brown on one side, turn, and brown on the other.

Ingredients

2 1/2   cups all-purpose flour
1/2   teaspoon salt
1/2   teaspoon baking soda
2   eggs
2   cups buttermilk

BUTTERMILK GRIDDLE CAKES

Your basic pancake. Hard to beat on a frosty Sunday morning.

MAKES ABOUT 8 LARGE PANCAKES.

Preparation

Preheat the oven to 425°. Sift the flour, salt, and soda together into a large bowl. Beat the eggs and mix with the buttermilk. Stir the liquids into the dry ingredients. Ladle onto a hot griddle and bake about 5 minutes.

1/2	winter squash
1	cup milk
2	eggs
1	cup cornmeal
1	cup all-purpose flour
1/2	teaspoon salt
1	teaspoon baking powder

SQUASH GRIDDLE CAKES

These are delicious for a winter supper with roast chicken or fried pork chops. You can bake the squash way ahead of time and scrape and purée it when the squash is cooled. The recipe's a breeze after that.

MAKES ABOUT 10 CAKES.

Preparation

Preheat the oven to 400°. Cut the squash in half and place cut side down on a baking sheet. Bake in the oven until completely tender, about 40 minutes. Cool. Scrape out the flesh, and mash or purée in the food processor. Measure out 1 cup of pulp. Use the remaining squash for soup or seasoned as a vegetable side dish.

Preheat the oven to 425°. Beat the cup of squash with the milk and eggs. Sift the dry ingredients together and add. Mix into a smooth batter. Spoon into small cakes on a heated griddle and bake in the oven for 10 minutes.

JOHNNY CAKE

Ingredients

1   cup buttermilk
1   egg, beaten
1/2 teaspoon salt
2   teaspoons sugar
1/2 teaspoon baking soda
6   tablespoons cornmeal
3   tablespoons all-purpose
    flour

Some people say that "Johnny" is actually a profoundly southern pronunciation of the word "journey." These were called "journey" cakes because they held well when packed for a journey.

Boasting both cornmeal and flour, Johnny cakes are very satisfying and good for breakfast, lunch, or dinner.

MAKES ABOUT 8 CAKES.

Preparation

Combine the ingredients in a medium bowl and mix until blended. Spoon the mixture into a hot griddle and cook each side until crispy brown.

BATTER BREAD

Ingredients

1   cup water
1   cup milk
1   cup cornmeal
2   tablespoons cold boiled rice
1   teaspoon salt
1   tablespoon melted butter
2   eggs, well beaten
1   teaspoon baking powder

This has a great texture. Good with stew or a bit of gravy. It's also nice with butter and sorghum for breakfast.

SERVES 8.

Preparation

Preheat the oven to 350°. Boil the water together with the milk. Pour over the cornmeal and rice. Add the remaining ingredients and pour into a greased baking dish. Bake until firm and serve very hot.

POPOVERS

Beautiful and delicious. I particularly like popovers with pot roast.

MAKES ABOUT 6 POPOVERS.

Ingredients

- ½ teaspoon salt
- 1 cup all-purpose flour
- 1 cup buttermilk
- 2 eggs
- 2 teaspoons melted shortening

Preparation

Preheat the oven to 425° and heat a greased popover pan. Mix the salt and flour in a medium bowl. Add the milk slowly, stirring out any lumps. Beat the eggs lightly and add to the batter. Add the melted shortening and beat very well. Fill the greased popover tins half full. Bake for 30 minutes.

WHOLE WHEAT BISCUITS

A pleasant change of pace, a little heavier than your basic biscuit. Particularly nice with honey.

MAKES ABOUT 18 BISCUITS.

Ingredients

- 3 cups whole wheat flour
- 1 teaspoon salt
- 4 teaspoons baking powder
- 3 tablespoons shortening
- 1 cup cream

Preparation

Preheat the oven to 425°. Sift the dry ingredients into a large bowl. Work in the shortening with the tips of your fingers. Quickly stir the cream in, making a soft dough. Roll ½-inch thick, cut, and place on a greased baking sheet. Bake about 10 minutes.

2 cups all-purpose flour

3/4 teaspoon salt

2 teaspoons baking powder

1/2 teaspoon baking soda

6 tablespoons shortening

3/4 cup buttermilk (or clabber cream)

BUTTERMILK BISCUITS

The real thing. The shortening makes them bake up light, and the buttermilk gives great flavor and silky texture.

MAKES 18 TO 20 SMALL BISCUITS.

Preparation

Preheat the oven to 425°. Sift together the dry ingredients in a large bowl. Work in the shortening with just your fingertips until it resembles cornmeal. Add the buttermilk or clabber, just enough to make a stiff dough. Knead the dough lightly, but do not over work. Roll or pat out on a floured board to ¼-inch to ½-inch thickness. Cut into rounds and place on an ungreased cookie sheet. Bake for 12 to 15 minutes, until lightly browned. Serve hot with butter .

CINNAMON BISCUIT SCRAPS

I used to live for biscuit scraps as a little girl. A fun treat. They smell marvelous while baking.

Preparation

Roll out the leftover scraps of biscuit dough as thinly as possible. Spread the dough with softened butter and sprinkle with cinnamon and sugar mixed together. Roll the dough up jelly roll style and slice off 1-inch pieces. Place on a greased cookie sheet and bake at 400° degrees for about 10 minutes.

2   sweet potatoes

2   cups all-purpose flour

2½ tablespoons baking powder

½   teaspoon baking soda

¾   teaspoon salt

3   tablespoons firmly packed
    brown sugar

1   teaspoon ground ginger

¼   teaspoon grated nutmeg

½   cup butter, melted

⅔   cup buttermilk

¼   cup raw sugar

SWEET POTATO BISCUITS

These taste very rich and sweat potato-ey, thanks to the baking of the sweet potatoes, which intensifies their flavor.

MAKES ABOUT 16 BISCUITS.

Preparation

Preheat the oven to 350°. Bake the sweet potatoes in their skins for about 30 minutes, until very soft. Peel and mash while still hot.

Turn the oven up to 400°. Sift together the dry ingredients and set aside. Place the mashed sweet potato in a mixing bowl and beat in the melted butter. Add the flour mixture and then the buttermilk. Don't over mix. The dough will be quite tacky. Pat down the dough to ½ inch on a floured board and cut out with a floured biscuit cutter. Sprinkle the tops with the raw sugar. Place on a greased cookie sheet and bake for about 20 minutes until browned. If the bottom begins to be too brown before the tops, turn the oven to broil and watch carefully until the tops are nicely browned. Serve with butter and sorghum or honey.

Ingredients

- 2 cups cornmeal
- 1/2 teaspoon baking soda
- 1 teaspoon salt
- 1 teaspoon baking powder
- 2 teaspoons sugar
- 1/2 cup all-purpose flour
- 2 eggs
- 2 cups buttermilk
- 1/2 cup vegetable oil

CORNMEAL WAFFLES

I love the texture of these. The outside gets really crispy and soaks up lots of maple syrup. These are also great for dinner with beef or turkey hash.

MAKES ABOUT 6 WAFFLES.

Preparation

Mix together the dry ingredients in a large bowl. Beat the eggs, combine with the buttermilk, and mix into the dry ingredients, stirring the oil in last. Pour the batter into a preheated waffle iron and cook until brown.

Ingredients

- 1 teaspoon salt
- 2 tablespoons cornmeal
- 1 teaspoon baking soda
- 1 teaspoon baking powder
- 4 cups all-purpose flour
- 2 eggs, beaten
- 2 cups buttermilk
- 2 tablespoons shortening, added last

WAFFLES

My sisters and I waged a continual battle over waffles with our grandmother, who believed that we were eating our waffles underdone. "Anemic looking," she called them. A true waffle lover herself, our anemic looking waffles upset her to no end. She shook her head in disgust and took her own waffle so brown that it was almost burnt. We complained that they scratched the tops of our mouths. Luckily there were always plenty of waffles to suit everyone.

MAKES ABOUT 8 LARGE WAFFLES.

Preparation

Sift the dry ingredients in a large bowl and set aside. Beat well the eggs and buttermilk in a separate bowl. Make a well in the dry ingredients and pour in the egg-buttermilk mixture. Pour in the melted shortening to combine. Pour into a preheated waffle iron and bake until golden. Turn onto a warm platter and brush with melted butter.

Ingredients

1	cup milk
1/3	cup butter
2/3	cup sugar
1	teaspoon salt
1	envelope yeast
2	eggs
	All-purpose flour
5	tart apples
1/4	cup sugar
1/2	teaspoon ground cinnamon
2	tablespoons currants
1/4	cup butter, melted

APPLE BREAKFAST CAKE

A very pretty breakfast cake for a special weekend. It can be made ahead and wrapped in foil to reheat, but it's not quite the same as serving it fresh.

SERVES 10.

Preparation

Scald the milk and mix together with shortening, sugar, and salt. Let cool to tepid and stir in the yeast. When the yeast has foamed, after about 5 minutes, beat in the eggs and enough flour to make a soft dough. Cover and let rise for 1 hour.

Beat down thoroughly, cover, and let rise again. Spread into a pan greased with shortening. Brush the top with melted butter.

Peel and core the apples and slice into eighths. Press the apple slices into the cake in 2 rows. Mix the sugar and cinnamon together and sprinkle over the top, along with the currants. Cover lightly and let rise another hour.

Bake in a preheated 350° oven for 30 minutes.

Ingredients

3 cups plus 1 cup whole wheat
  flour
1/2 cup nonfat dry milk
1 tablespoon salt
2 packages dry yeast
3 cups water
1/2 cup honey
2 tablespoons vegetable oil
3 cups all-purpose flour (or
  more as needed)

HONEY WHOLE WHEAT BREAD

Mama started making this bread when I was a preteen. I used to go on long winter walks through the hills around Radnor Lake and come home to find a fire in the kitchen fireplace, the tea kettle on the stove, and the bread fresh out of the oven with a knife and butter waiting. Definitely worth coming home to.

MAKES 2 MEDIUM LOAVES.

Preparation

Grease 2 9 x 5-inch loaf pans. Combine 3 cups of whole wheat flour, dry milk, salt and yeast together in a large bowl. Heat the water, honey, and vegetable oil over low heat to just warm. Pour the warm liquid over the dry ingredients and mix with an electric mixer for about 3 minutes.

Add the additional whole wheat flour and all-purpose flour and stir in by hand. Turn out onto a floured board and knead for 5 minutes. Place the dough in a greased bowl. Cover and let rise until doubles in bulk, about 45 minutes to 1 hour.

Punch down the dough and divide in half. Using a rolling pin, roll each half into a rectangle. Roll up like a jelly roll, starting from one of the shorter ends, and place the rolled dough in greased loaf pans. Cover and let rise until doubled, about 40 minutes.

Bake in a preheated 375° oven for approximately 45 minutes until the loaf sounds hollow when lightly tapped.

Turn the bread out of the pans and cool on a wire rack before slicing.

Ingredients

- 2 cups milk
- 1/4 cup butter
- 1/4 cup shortening
- 3 cups plus 3 cups all-purpose flour
- 1 teaspoon salt
- 1 package dry yeast

GRANDMAMA'S WHITE BREAD

Whole wheat flour was considered rather coarse in my grandmother's day, while white flour was obviously refined, literally and figuratively. Of coarse this won't win any nutrition awards, but the taste and texture are divine. Such a treat toasted and buttered for breakfast.

MAKES 2 MEDIUM LOAVES.

Preparation

Scald the milk and pour over the butter and shortening. Let cool to just warm. Mix 3 cups of flour, the salt, and yeast together in a large mixing bowl and pour the warm milk mixture over. Beat together for 3 minutes. Turn dough into a greased bowl, cover, and let rise until for about 1 hour and 30 minutes, until double.

Beat in the additional flour (if the dough seems too sticky add up to 1 cup more) and knead for 5 minutes. Again, place in a greased bowl and let rise for about 2 hours until doubled.

Divide and shape into 2 loaves, place in greased loaf pans, and let rise about 2 more hours until doubled.

Bake at 350° for 40 minutes, until nicely browned and the loaf sounds hollow when tapped. Turn out onto a wire rack to cool before slicing.

Ingredients

½ cup water
½ cup shortening
¼ cup sugar
1 teaspoon salt
1 package yeast
Pinch sugar
1 egg
3 cups all-purpose flour
1 teaspoon or so shortening
¼ cup butter, melted

YEAST ROLLS

This is Mama's recipe for the rolls that have always graced our dining room table for family parties. Mama gets a second pan of hot rolls out of the oven about midway through dinner, and insists that we spread on lots of butter.

MAKES ENOUGH DOUGH FOR ABOUT 72 SMALL ROLLS.

Preparation

Heat the water and ½ cup of shortening together in a saucepan to melt the shortening. Place the ¼ cup of sugar and the salt in a large bowl and pour the water and shortening over. Dissolve the yeast with the pinch of sugar in ¼ cup lukewarm water in a small bowl. If the yeast doesn't start to react within a minute, throw it out. Your yeast is probably dead, and you need some fresh yeast. The yeast should start to foam and spore. Let the yeast sit for 5 minutes, then add to the water and shortening mixture and stir. Beat the egg into the mixture and stir in the flour. Form into a ball and grease the top of the dough with 1 teaspoon of shortening. Let rise for 1 hour.

After the dough has risen, cover and set in the refrigerator until you're ready to use, up to 2 days.

Lightly grease 2 baking sheets. Roll out the dough and cut in small circles. Dip in the melted butter and place, folded into a half-circle, on a greased baking sheet. Let rise for 2 hours.

Bake the rolls in a preheated 375° oven for 10 to 15 minutes until lightly browned and risen.

HOT CROSS BUNS

MAKES 24 BUNS.

Preparation

To modify the Yeast Roll recipe into hot cross buns, simply add ½ teaspoon more sugar and 1 teaspoon of cinnamon. Add 1 cup of currants with the flour. After the dough has risen for 1 hour, divide into 24 even pieces. Dip these into butter and flatten slightly as you press them onto a greased baking sheet. Use scissors or a sharp knife to snip a small cross in the top of each bun and let rise for 2 hours. Bake about 5 to 10 minutes longer than rolls. Remove from the oven and ice lightly with an icing made of confectioners' sugar, milk, and a bit of vanilla.

Ingredients

½	pound dates, chopped
½	pound crystallized ginger, chopped
1½	cups water
2	teaspoons baking soda
2	eggs
1½	cups sugar
2	tablespoons butter, melted
3½	cups all-purpose flour
¾	teaspoon salt
1	teaspoon vanilla extract
1	cup sliced walnuts

GINGER DATE NUT BREAD

I adore the zingy taste of ginger, wonderful with the dates. Spread this bread with sweet butter or a little cream cheese.

MAKES 1 MEDIUM LOAF.

Preparation

Preheat the oven to 300°. Grease a 9 x 5-inch loaf pan. Place the dates and ginger together in a mixing bowl. Boil the water with the soda and pour over the dates and ginger. Stir and allow the mixture to cool. Beat the eggs and sugar together and add, mixing well, along with the melted butter. Sift the flour with the salt and stir into the batter. Add the vanilla and walnuts and combine. Pour into the prepared loaf pan. Bake for 1 hour.

Ingredients

- ⅔ cup butter, softened
- 1⅓ cups sugar
- 2 eggs
- 3 to 4 bananas (1½ cups mashed banana)
- 3 cups all-purpose flour
- 1 teaspoon baking soda
- 1 teaspoon baking powder
- ⅓ cup buttermilk, clabber, or sour cream
- 1 teaspoon vanilla extract
- 1 cup chopped black walnuts

BANANA BREAD WITH BLACK WALNUTS

I love the flavor of black walnuts, which grow wild in the mid-South. Some people find them a little overpowering. Substitute English walnuts, if you choose. The buttermilk makes this a moist and silky bread.

MAKES 1 LARGE LOAF.

Preparation

Preheat the oven to 350°. Grease and flour 1 large or 2 small loaf pans. Cream the butter and the sugar and mix in the eggs, beating until light. Sift the dry ingredients and mix into the batter. Mix in the bananas and then the buttermilk, stirring just to blend. Fold in the walnuts and pour the batter into the prepared pan(s). Bake for 1 hour and 30 minutes for a large pan or 1 hour for the small.

Ingredients

- 1 cup butter
- 1½ cups sugar
- Grated zest and 1 teaspoon juice from 1 lemon
- 4 eggs
- 3 cups all-purpose flour
- 1 teaspoon salt
- ½ teaspoon baking soda
- 1 cup strawberry jam
- 1 cup chopped walnuts
- ½ cup sour cream

STRAWBERRY BREAD

This is a nice gooey, sweet bread. Really great toasted.

MAKES 2 LOAVES.

Preparation

Preheat the oven to 325°. Grease and flour 2 medium loaf pans. Cream the butter with the sugar and lemon juice, beating until light. Add the eggs and beat well. Sift together the flour, salt, and soda, and mix in. Mix together the jam, nuts, and sour cream and fold into the batter. Pour the batter into the prepared loaf pans and bake for almost 1 hour, until a straw inserted in the center comes out clean. Cool in the pans for 10 minutes before turning out on wires to cool completely.

1   pound cranberries

2   cups all-purpose flour

2½ cups sugar

1   tablespoon baking powder

2   teaspoons salt

1   teaspoon baking soda

    Juice and zest from 2
      oranges

    Juice and zest from 2 limes

2   eggs

¼   cup shortening

¼   cup water

2   cups chopped walnuts

CRANBERRY LOAF

Tangy in flavor and truly beautiful. A lovely present.

MAKES 2 MEDIUM LOAVES.

Preparation

Preheat the oven to 325°. Grease and flour 2 medium loaf pans. Rinse and dry the cranberries and roughly chop by hand. Sift together the dry ingredients in a medium bowl. Zest the oranges and limes before juicing. Measure the orange and lime juice to make 1 cup. Add more orange juice, if necessary. Beat the eggs in a large bowl. Melt the shortening and boil the water separately and mix these together with the juice. Pour the liquid into the eggs, beating. Add the dry ingredients, beating slowly until smooth. Fold in the cranberries, fruit zests, and walnuts. Fill the prepared loaf pans two-thirds full with the batter. Bake for 45 minutes, or until a straw inserted in the center comes out clean.

PUMPKIN BREAD

The buttermilk and pumpkin combine to give a satiny smooth texture to this bread.

MAKES 2 MEDIUM LOAVES.

Ingredients

1½   cups sugar
2/3   cup shortening
4   eggs
2   cups puréed pumpkin
2/3   cup buttermilk
1   tablespoon bourbon
3½   cups all-purpose flour
½   teaspoon baking powder
2   teaspoons baking soda
2   teaspoons salt
2   teaspoons ground cinnamon
½   teaspoon grated nutmeg
1   cup chopped pecans

Preparation

Preheat the oven to 350°. Grease and flour 2 medium loaf pans. Cream together the sugar and shortening in a large bowl. Beat in the egg until fluffy. Mix in the pumpkin, buttermilk, and bourbon. Sift together the dry ingredients and add to the batter, blending well. Fold in the nuts. Pour into the prepared pans. Bake for 1 hour until a straw inserted in the center comes out clean.

LEMON TEA BREAD

Delicate flavor and light texture. Just right with tea.

MAKES 1 MEDIUM LOAF.

Ingredients

½   cup butter
1   cup sugar
2   eggs
1½   cups all-purpose flour
1   teaspoon baking powder
1   teaspoon salt
½   cup buttermilk
3   lemons, zested and juiced
½   cup ground almonds

Preparation

Preheat the oven to 325°. Grease and flour a medium loaf pan. Cream the butter with the sugar. Add the eggs and beat until light. Sift the dry ingredients and mix in. Stir in the buttermilk, then the lemon juice and zest, and ground almonds. Pour the batter into the prepared pan. Bake for 50 minutes or until a straw inserted in the center comes out clean.

While the bread is baking, stir together the juice of 1 additional lemon with ½ cup of sugar. Remove the baked bread from the oven and use a straw or skewer to poke several holes in the top. Pour the lemon and sugar over and let the bread sit in the pan for at least 1 hour before removing.

Chapter 11

CAKES, CANDIES, AND COOKIES

❧

*I*t's a challenge to find a Southerner without a sweet tooth. How could you help but develop a fondness for desserts when you're constantly surrounded by such temptation? Rarely a dinner and very few lunches went by in my family without the promise of something sweet to round it all off. In fact, sometimes dessert seemed to be the main event and dinner merely an obligatory exercise through which we hurried.

And of course there were the mandatory snacks after school. When I was very young, before Mother began to teach and she and I were at home, we would prepare for my sisters' daily return on the school bus as if we were celebrating the homecoming of the prodigal daughters who'd been years away roaming the countryside. Fresh baked cookies, popcorn balls, or fudge—something sweet and freshly cooked was waiting on the kitchen table by three o'clock sharp. Luckily Mother stressed sharing with our neighborhood pals, or we all would have been more plump than pleasing.

I believe that the most exciting array of desserts I've ever seen was that which ladened the tables of our church picnics. Here the cooks all labored to out-do themselves and each other with gooey, rich, homemade pies and tarts, towering cakes, pans of brownies, and trays of chewy cookies, all about eye level with the clusters of wandering children who had no intention of waiting until after dinner to satisfy their sweet longings. Desserts, it seems, have always been a part of our scenery.

"Cake baking is an art which may be acquired through industry and accuracy."
—Kate Brew Vaughn, 1914

Cakes are serious stuff. You have to be on your toes. You have to measure, weigh, and calculate. You cannot just feel your way around a cake. But what a magnificent show of devotion or of celebration we have with the finished product. What other food gets borne into a room alight with candles, festooned with flowers, accompanied by song? I mean, no matter how much we love it, I've never heard people break out in chorus when a platter of fried chicken was brought to the table. Never seen anyone stick a candle into a tomato sandwich and light it. Cakes are the chosen culinary element that marks all of the "big" events of our lives. The birthdays, weddings, and anniversaries. So cakes are serious stuff deserving of our concentration, certainly worthy of fresh products and maybe a little hand mixing. I'll even put my glasses on to read the measuring cup.

1   cup butter
2   cups sugar
4   eggs, separated
3   cups all-purpose flour
1   tablespoon baking powder
½   teaspoon salt
1   cup milk
2   teaspoons vanilla extract

1-2-3-4 CAKE

This is the standard cake from which many fancies may depart. By a simple frosting it can suddenly be transformed into strawberry cake, coconut cake, or just a great yellow cake with chocolate icing. Hard to beat.

1-2-3-4 refers to the measurements of butter, sugar, flour, and eggs. Hard to forget as well.

SERVES 8 TO 12.

Preparation

Preheat the oven to 350°. Grease 2 9-inch cake pans with shortening and dust with flour. Set aside.

Cream the butter with the sugar to a light consistency. Add the yolks one at a time, beating well after each addition.

Sift together the dry ingredients and mix into the batter. Add the milk and vanilla, mixing well. Beat the egg whites stiff and fold into the batter.

Pour into the prepared cake pans and bake for about 30 minutes, until a skewer inserted in the center comes out clean.

Cool for several minutes in the pan. Turn the cakes out onto wire racks and cool completely. Cakes may be wrapped and frozen.

Ingredients

1	fresh coconut
⅔	cup water
2	cups sugar
1	egg white
1	dozen marshmallows

COCONUT ICING

MAKES FROSTING FOR 1 TWO-LAYER CAKE.

Preparation

Crack open the coconut and save the milk. While the cakes are cooling, pour the coconut milk evenly over both layers. Grate the coconut meat and reserve.

Boil the water and sugar together to 238°. While the syrup is cooking, beat the egg white stiff. When the syrup reaches temperature, pour into the beaten egg white in a thin, steady stream, beating constantly. Stir in the marshmallows, stirring until cool enough to spread. Stir in the reserved coconut and and ice between the layers, along the sides, and over the top of the cake.

Ingredients

1	cup fresh strawberries
1¼	cups sugar
1	egg white
⅛	teaspoon salt

STRAWBERRY ICING

MAKES ABOUT 2¼ CUPS.

Preparation

Rinse and hull the strawberries. Place in a mixing bowl and pour the sugar over the berries. Add the egg white and salt, and beat on high with an electric mixer for 10 minutes, until light and stiff. This icing is beautiful and delicious, but must be used and eaten the day it is made.

Ingredients

- 2 **egg yolks**
- ¼ **cup milk, scalded**
- 2¼ **cups confectioners' sugar**
- 1 **tablespoon vanilla extract**
- 2 **ounces unsweetened chocolate**
- 1 **tablespoon butter**

CHOCOLATE ICING

MAKES ICING FOR 1 TWO-LAYER OR SHEET CAKE.

Preparation

Beat the egg yolks. Add the milk, sugar, and vanilla. Beat well. Melt the chocolate with the butter in the top of a double boiler over simmering water. Pour the chocolate and butter into the egg mixture and mix. Let cool to spreading consistency.

Ingredients

- ½ **cup butter**
- ½ **cup sugar**
- ½ **cup dark molasses**
- 2 **eggs, well beaten**
- ½ **cup milk**
- ½ **teaspoon salt**
- 1 **teaspoon baking soda**
- 2 **teaspoons ground ginger**
- 2½ **cups all-purpose flour**

GINGER CAKE

Such a comfort, ginger cake. It takes the chill right out of the air.

SERVES 4 TO 6.

Preparation

Preheat the oven to 350°. Cream the butter with the sugar. Beat in the molasses and then the eggs and milk. Sift together the dry ingredients and mix in well. Pour into a greased loaf pan and bake for 40 minutes, until a tester inserted in the center comes out clean.

Let cool slightly and turn out onto wire racks. Serve warm with whipped cream.

CARAMEL CAKE

Around these parts a "caramel cake" is frequently a white cake with caramel icing. This cake is really caramel, with real caramel in it. Don't be frightened. You can do this, and you'll love it.

SERVES 8 TO 12.

Ingredients

½ cup sugar
½ cup boiling water

½ cup butter
1½ cups sugar
2 eggs, separated
3 cups all-purpose flour
2 teaspoons baking powder
1 cup milk
1 teaspoon vanilla extract

Preparation

Place the sugar in a heavy saucepan over medium high heat and stir constantly until it begins to melt and brown. Remove from the fire and pour in the boiling water, stirring like crazy. Return to the the heat and stir until you have a thick syrup. Set aside.

Preheat the oven to 350°. Grease 2 9-inch cake pans with shortening and dust with flour. Cream the butter with the sugar and beat in the egg yolks. Sift together the dry ingredients and mix in alternating with the milk, in 2 additions. Add the vanilla extract and 3 tablespoons of caramel and mix well. Beat the egg whites stiff and fold in. Pour into the prepared cake pans and bake for about 30 minutes until a tester inserted comes out clean. Cool in the pans for several minutes, then turn out onto wire racks, and let cakes cool completely. Ice with Boiled White Icing.

BOILED WHITE ICING

MAKES ICING FOR 1 TWO-LAYER CAKE.

Ingredients

1 cup water
2 cups plus ¼ cup sugar
1 tablespoon light corn syrup
3 egg whites, at room temperature
1 teaspoon vanilla extract

Preparation

Boil the water and pour in the 2 cups of sugar and corn syrup. Boil hard until it reaches soft ball stage (240°).

While the syrup is boiling, beat the whites foamy, sprinkle in ¼ cup of sugar, and beat until very stiff, almost dry. When the syrup reaches temperature, pour it into the side of the bowl of the egg whites in a thin steady stream, beating like mad until all syrup is incorporated. Beat in the vanilla and cool slightly before icing the cake. Do not overcool or the icing will become brittle.

SPICE CAKE

Really a spice cake, with even a subtle bit of cayenne. This is an old, old recipe.

SERVES 8 TO 12.

Ingredients

- 1   cup butter
- 2   cups firmly packed brown sugar
- 7   egg yolks
- 1   egg
- 1   cup buttermilk
- 1   cup molasses
- 5   cups all-purpose flour
- 1   teaspoon baking soda
- 1   teaspoon ground cloves
- 2   teaspoons ground ginger
- 2   teaspoons ground cinnamon
- 1   teaspoon grated nutmeg
- 1/4 teaspoon cayenne pepper

Preparation

Preheat the oven to 350°. Grease 2 9-inch round cake pans. Cream together the butter and the sugar. Beat in the eggs, beating to a light batter. Mix in the buttermilk and molasses. Sift together the flour and soda and mix in. Finally, mix in all of the spices. Pour into the prepared cake pans and bake for about 30 minutes, until a tester inserted in the center comes out clean.

Let cool in the pans for 10 minutes. Turn out onto wire racks and cool completely. Put together and ice with Caramel Icing (recipe follows).

CARAMEL ICING

MAKES ICING FOR 1 TWO-LAYER CAKE.

Ingredients

- 1   pound light brown sugar
- 3   tablespoons all-purpose flour
- 3/4 cup cold water
- 1/2 cup butter
- 1   16-ounce box confectioners' sugar, sifted
- 1   teaspoon vanilla extract

Preparation

Mix together the brown sugar, flour, water, and butter in a saucepan off the heat. Dissolve thoroughly and cook to about 236°, just under the soft ball stage. Remove from the heat and cool without stirring for 10 minutes.

Add the confectioners' sugar and vanilla and beat to a spreading consistency. If it gets too stiff, thin it with a little cream or milk.

Ingredients

- ½ cup shortening
- 1½ cups sugar
- 3 cups all-purpose flour
- 3 teaspoons baking powder
- 1 teaspoon salt
- 1 cup water
- 1 teaspoon vanilla extract
- 4 egg whites

GRANDMAMA'S PINEAPPLE CAKE

Actually, a white cake with pineapple icing. This cake appeared on the cut glass cake stand for special occasions like birthdays. Grandmama liked to tie ribbon around coins and slide them under the cake for children to pull out. That way everyone got a favor.

SERVES 8 TO 12.

Preparation

Preheat the oven to 350°. Grease and flour 2 9-inch cake pans. Cream together the shortening and sugar. Sift the dry ingredients and add alternately with the water. Add the vanilla and beat thoroughly. Beat the egg whites stiff and fold into the batter. Pour into 2 greased 9-inch cake tins and bake for 20 minutes, until a tester inserted in the center comes out clean.

Let cool in the pans for 10 minutes before turning out onto racks and cooling entirely.

Ingredients

- 1 8¼-ounce can crushed pineapple
- ⅔ cup water
- 2 cups sugar
- 1 egg white
- 1 dozen marshmallows

PINEAPPLE ICING

MAKES ICING FOR 1 TWO-LAYER CAKE.

Preparation

Drain the pineapple very well, reserving the juice. While the cakes are cooling, pour the juice from the pineapple over both layers. Set the pineapple aside.

Boil the water and sugar together to 238° (soft ball). While that is cooking, beat the egg white stiff. Pour the syrup over the egg white in a thin stream, beating. Add the marshmallows and beat until cool. Fold in the well-drained pineapple. Spread the icing between the layers, on the sides, and over the top of the stacked cakes. If the icing is too runny, beat in confectioners' sugar until it thickens enough to cling to the cake.

BLACKBERRY JAM CAKE

A yummy old fashioned dessert. Slightly chewy and plenty sweet. Great with a cold, cold glass of milk.

SERVES 8 TO 12.

Ingredients

- 1 cup butter
- 2 cups sugar
- 5 eggs, separated
- 1 cup buttermilk
- 4 cups all-purpose flour
- 2 teaspoons baking soda
- 2 teaspoons ground cinnamon
- 2 cups blackberry jam

Preparation

Preheat the oven to 350°. Grease 2 9-inch cake pans with shortening and dust with flour. Set aside.

Cream the butter with the sugar. Beat in the egg yolks one at a time, and then the buttermilk. Sift together the flour, soda, and cinnamon, and mix in. Stir in the jam. Beat the egg whites stiff and fold in. Pour the batter into the prepared cake pans and bake for about 30 minutes, until a tester comes out clean. Spread with caramel icing.

FUDGE CAKE

This is yummy, gooey, and chocolatey, and can be made in one pan in a matter of minutes.

MAKES ABOUT 12 SQUARES.

Ingredients

- ½ cup butter
- 1 cup sugar
- 1½ squares chocolate
- ¾ cup all-purpose flour
- ¼ teaspoon salt
- ¼ teaspoon baking powder
- 2 eggs
- 1 teaspoon vanilla extract
- 1 cup broken walnuts

Preparation

Preheat the oven to 325°. Grease and flour a 9-inch square baking pan.

Melt the butter, sugar, and chocolate together. Sift the flour, salt, and baking powder into this. Add the eggs, vanilla, and nuts. Mix well and pour into the prepared pan. Bake for 35 minutes.

Let cool completely. This is very rich and delicious as is. My mother likes to ice it with a dark chocolate frosting, sending the choco-meter way over the top.

STRAWBERRY SHORTCAKE

Ingredients

2 quarts strawberries
½ cup sugar

1 pint heavy cream
3 tablespoons confectioners' sugar

2 cups all-purpose flour
4 teaspoons baking powder
1 teaspoon salt
2½ teaspoons firmly packed light brown sugar
⅓ cup shortening
⅔ cup buttermilk
1 tablespoon melted butter

This is, in my humble opinion, the best dessert ever created by anyone ever in the history of the world. I believe it must be one of Mama's favorite's, too, because every year on at least one Sunday during the early summer, Mama would serve our family of five an entire strawberry shortcake for lunch after Sunday school. No veggies, no meat, just one fifth of a cake per person.

As the high school dishwashers at work taught me to say, "Mom rocks." So does the cake.

SERVES 6 TO 8.

Preparation

Rinse, hull, and slice the strawberries, reserving about 12 good-looking ones for the top of the cake. Place the sliced berries in a bowl and pour the sugar over. Stir well and even mash a little. Set aside.

Whip the cream with the confectioners' sugar to hold soft peaks. Refrigerate while you make the shortcake.

Preheat the oven to 425°. Sift together the flour, baking powder, salt, and brown sugar. Use your fingertips to work in the shortening until the mixture resembles cornmeal. Add the buttermilk and butter, and mix to a soft dough. Roll out on a floured board to ½-inch thickness. Use a 9-inch cake pan as a "cutter," making 2 circles. Grease the inside of 2 cake pans and place the dough loosely inside. Bake for 30 or so minutes, until cooked through. Turn out the shortcakes and place one on a serving platter. Spread with butter. Spread about two-thirds of the macerated berries on top. Place the other cake over this. Top with the remaining macerated berries and lightly spread or spoon the whipped cream over. Top with the reserved whole berries and serve immediately.

This gets a little sloppy, but that's half the fun. It's a luxurious kind of sloppiness. Use this with any summer fruit: blackberries, plums, peaches, cherries, blueberries, raspberries, and any combination thereof. Don't let the shortcake cool too much before serving. I love the warmth of the cake with the cool cream and refreshing berries.

1 cup all-purpose flour

1/2 cup confectioners' sugar

1/2 teaspoon salt

3/4 cup superfine sugar

12 egg whites, at room temperature

1 teaspoon cream of tartar

1 teaspoon vanilla extract

1 teaspoon almond extract

ANGEL FOOD CAKE

A virtually fat-free dessert which, amazingly enough, tastes divine. I guess that's where they get the name.

SERVES 8 TO 12.

Preparation

Preheat the oven to 325°. Have ready an ungreased standard bundt pan. Sift the flour with the confectioners' sugar and salt. Set aside. Sift the superfine sugar and set aside.

Place the whites in a mixing bowl and use an electric mixer to beat the whites on low until frothy. Add the cream of tartar and continue beating. Gradually add the superfine sugar with the mixer running. Whip until almost stiff. The whites should have a high sheen. Fold in the almond and vanilla by hand with a whisk. Gradually fold in the flour mixture with a rubber spatula, just folding in and not over mixing. Be sure to scrape down to the bottom of the bowl as you go.

Pour the batter into the tube pan. Gently tap the pan on the work surface to release any air bubbles. Place in the center of the oven and bake for 45 minutes, until well risen and golden brown.

Remove from the oven and set upside down, inverted through the funnel onto a bottle. Let the cake sit that way until completely cooled, up to several hours.

Slice into large wedges and serve with fresh fruit and whipped cream, lemon curd, or raspberry sauce.

1 pound butter

1 pound sugar

10 eggs, separated

2 tablespoons whiskey

1 teaspoon vanilla extract

1 pound all-purpose flour (4 cups)

½ teaspoon salt

POUND CAKE

Oh my goodness, I do love pound cake. I sneak chunks of it and eat it plain. I toast pound cake and proclaim it breakfast. I add whipped cream and berries for a fancy dessert.

Pound cake is so-called because of the recipe, which calls for a pound of fat, a pound of sugar, and a pound flour. Easy to remember. Actually hard to forget. A thousand variations have been created upon the theme. This recipe is a very old-fashioned one with no leavening except for the eggs. It makes a simple, dense, and decadent cake.

SERVES 8 TO 12.

Preparation

Preheat the oven to 325°. Grease and lightly flour 2 medium loaf pans. Cream the butter well, add the sugar and cream until light and fluffy. Beat the egg yolks and mix in until very light. Stir in the whiskey and vanilla. Sift together the flour and salt and stir in. Beat the egg whites to soft peaks. Gently fold into the batter until just blended. Turn into the loaf pans and bake for 1 hour, or when the cake springs to the touch.

Cool in the pans for 10 minutes before turning out onto wire racks to cool thoroughly.

1 pound white raisins

½ pound citron, chopped

½ pound candied cherries, chopped

½ pound candied pineapple, chopped

¼ pound orange peel

¼ pound lemon peel

½ cup sherry

1 cup butter

2 cups sugar

3½ cups all-purpose flour

3 teaspoons baking powder

½ teaspoon salt

1 cup milk

6 egg whites

1 cup coconut

½ pound almonds

½ pound pecans

FRUIT CAKE

He who dislikes fruitcake has never had my mother's, or at least never helped her make it. This was one of several cooking productions performed in our household just prior to Christmas, in which we all took part. My older sisters got to cut out the paper to line the pans, and I was assigned the task of greasing the paper. I eventually graduated to the stature of fruit chopper after my sisters had deserted us for other pursuits.

This is a very special gift to receive, delightful to nibble on with a spot of sherry on a bitter cold afternoon. The store bought kind just misses the point, and the taste.

MAKES 7 ONE-POUND LOAVES, OR APPROXIMATELY 4 TUBE CAKES.

Preparation

Soak the chopped fruit in the sherry overnight.

Line baking pans (tube pans or loaves) with greased brown paper (we used grocery bags) or parchment. Preheat the oven to 325°.

Cream together the butter and sugar. Sift the dry ingredients together and add alternately with the milk. Beat the egg whites stiff and fold in. Stir in the coconut, almonds, pecans, and fruit.

Pour into the prepared pans and bake until a straw inserted in the center comes out clean. Pour the remaining sherry over while the cakes are still warm in the pans. Let the cakes cool in the pans before turning out.

½   cup butter
1½ cups firmly packed brown
    sugar
2   eggs
1½ cups self-rising flour
1   teaspoon vanilla extract
1   cup chopped pecans or
    walnuts

BUTTERSCOTCH BROWNIES

MAKES 8 SERVINGS.

Preparation

Preheat the oven to 350°. Grease a 9 x 13-inch pan. Melt butter in a saucepan. Add sugar and bring to a boil over low heat, stirring constantly. Remove from heat and let cool for ten minutes. Beat in the eggs, one at a time. Add the flour and vanilla and stir well. Fold in the nuts and pour into the prepared pan. Bake for 35 minutes. Let cool before cutting.

1   cup all-purpose flour
¼   cup confectioners' sugar
½   cup butter

    Juice and grated zest from 3
    lemons
1   cup sugar
2   eggs, lightly beaten
2   tablespoons all-purpose
    flour

LEMON SQUARES

MAKES 8 SERVINGS.

Preparation

Preheat the oven to 350°. Mix together the flour and sugar. Cut the butter in bits and mix in just until the mixture will cling together. Press into the bottom of a 9-inch square pan and bake for 10 minutes, while you prepare the filling.

Zest the lemons before you juice them. Beat the sugar into the eggs and stir in the other ingredients. Pour over the pre-baked bottom layer and cook for 20 minutes longer, until set.

DIVINITY FUDGE

Smooth and very, very sweet. A nice present for the holidays.

SERVES 6 TO 8

Ingredients

2 egg whites
2½ cups sugar
½ cup light corn syrup
½ cup water
1½ cups chopped pecans
½ teaspoon vanilla extract

Preparation

B eat the egg whites stiff. Set aside

Mix the sugar, corn syrup, and water in a heavy saucepan. Cook on medium-high heat, stirring constantly, until the soft ball stage is reached. Test by putting 1 or 2 drops in cold water. This should hold a ball that will remain soft when rolled between your fingers. A candy thermometer should register 235°.

Pour half of the mixture over the stiff egg whites. Return the pan to the heat and continue cooking to the hard ball stage (250° on a candy thermometer).

Add the egg white mixture along with the nuts and vanilla and stir together. Spread onto a buttered dish. Cut the fudge before it completely sets.

PEANUT BUTTER FUDGE

Rich and silky.

SERVES 8.

Ingredients

3 cups sugar
3 tablespoons light corn syrup
½ cup peanut butter
1¼ cups whole milk
2 tablespoons butter
2 teaspoons vanilla extract

Preparation

B utter a 7x11-inch pan. In a large heavy saucepan combine the sugar, corn syrup, peanut butter, and milk. Stir well. Cook over medium heat to soft ball stage. Remove from the heat and add the peanut butter and vanilla. Beat until the mixture is thick and has lost its gloss. Pour into the prepared pan. Let cool and cut into squares.

1½ cups sugar
½ cup light corn syrup
¼ teaspoon salt
3 tablespoons cold water
2 cups raw shelled peanuts
1 teaspoon baking soda

PEANUT BRITTLE

This is easy and makes a great holiday present.

SERVES 6 TO 8.

Preparation

Grease a cookie sheet with shortening. Set aside.

Combine all of the ingredients except the peanuts in a heavy 1-quart saucepan and bring to a rolling boil. Pour in the peanuts. Keep at a rolling boil and stir the peanuts until they begin to pop and the syrup is a golden amber. Remove from the stove and stir in the soda. Beat until well mixed. Pour onto the prepared cookie sheet and let cool. Break into pieces.

Ingredients

3 pounds caramel candies
½ cup evaporated milk
12 super-crisp apples

CARAMEL APPLES

Surprise! I use the easy way! It happens to be the best.

SERVES 12.

Preparation

Place the candies and milk in a deep saucepan and melt over low heat, stirring occasionally, until melted and creamy.

While those are heating, rinse the apples and use wooden sucker sticks to pierce through the core of each apple.

Stand each apple in the pan with the caramel and spoon the caramel over the apple.

Rest the caramel apples on wax paper and chill to harden the caramel.

6 quarts popped corn

2 cups sugar

1½ cups water

½ teaspoon salt

½ cup light corn syrup

1 teaspoon vinegar

1 teaspoon vanilla extract

POPCORN BALLS

A Halloween necessity. Mama had us helping her to make these as little, little girls. She always buttered our hands to coat us against the hot candy. We realized that we were performing a dangerous but vital duty and took our jobs very seriously.

MAKES ABOUT 24 BALLS.

Preparation

Shake the popped corn in a bowl and remove any unpopped kernels that could prove hazardous to the teeth.

Combine the sugar, water, salt, corn syrup, vinegar, and vanilla in a saucepan. Bring to a boil and cook to the hard ball stage (250°). Pour the sugar mixture over the corn and stir. Butter your hands to press the mixture into balls while still hot. Be careful, and remember it is hot.

Grated zest and juice from 4 oranges

2 cups sugar

2 pounds pecan halves

½ teaspoon salt

¼ teaspoon cayenne pepper

1 teaspoon ground cinnamon

ORANGE CANDIED PECANS

Sweet? Savory? Well, a little of both. Great with cocktails, or to finish a grand meal.

SERVES 6 TO 8.

Preparation

Grate the zest from the oranges and then juice. Pour into a non-reactive saucepan along with the sugar and cook to 240°, the soft ball stage. Place the pecan halves in a bowl and sprinkle the salt, cayenne, and cinnamon over. Pour the candy over this and stir. Turn onto a cookie sheet and let cool. Break apart when cool enough to handle.

PRALINES

This is a softer praline than most folks are used to. They melt in your mouth.

MAKES ABOUT 2 DOZEN.

Ingredients

2½ cups sugar
1 cup milk
3 tablespoons butter
Vanilla extract
1 cup nuts

Preparation

Boil a scant 2 cups sugar with the milk. Melt the rest of the sugar in a heavy saucepan on top of the stove, stirring to avoid burning. When it begins to boil, pour in the milk and sugars. Cook, stirring, until it forms a ball. Add the butter, vanilla, and nuts, mixing well. Drop by spoonfuls onto waxed paper and allow to cool.

TOLL HOUSE COOKIES

A crispy chocolate chip cookie. Grandmother considered the chewy version "raw." This, she assured me, was a chocolate chip cookie to be proud of.

MAKES ABOUT 3 DOZEN COOKIES.

Ingredients

1 cup butter
¾ cup sugar
¾ cup firmly packed dark
   brown sugar
2 eggs
2¼ cups all-purpose flour
1 teaspoon baking soda
½ teaspoon salt
1 teaspoon vanilla extract
2½ teaspoons water
1 12-ounce package chocolate
   chips

Preparation

Cream the butter with the sugars and beat in the eggs. Sift together the flour, soda, and salt, and add to the sugar mixture. Mix thoroughly. Add the vanilla and water and mix thoroughly. Stir in the chocolate chips. Refrigerate for about 30 minutes.

Preheat the oven to 350°. Drop the mixture by teaspoonfuls onto a greased cookie sheet and bake for about 10 minutes. They are best slightly undercooked. Let cool on the baking sheet before trying to remove.

Ingredients

1 cup sugar
1 cup butter
2 eggs
2¼ cups all-purpose flour
1 teaspoon almond extract

MARY MELL CLEMENTS' SUGAR COOKIES

I found this recipe in my grandmother's notes. My mother tells me that Mary Mell is alive and well and a member of her study group. She just turned ninety.

I like to sprinkle the tops of these with granulated sugar and almond pieces

MAKES ABOUT 4 DOZEN COOKIES.

Preparation

Cream the sugar with the butter and beat in the eggs. Mix in the flour and almond extract. Mix thoroughly and chill before baking.

Preheat the oven to 350°. The dough may be rolled and cut out or formed into a log and sliced in ¼-inch circles. Bake on ungreased cookie sheet for 10 minutes, until the edges begin to brown. If you are topping with almonds, be careful that they don't get too brown—they can burn before you know it.

Ingredients

1 8-ounce can almond paste
1 cup sugar
3 unbeaten egg whites
¼ cup all-purpose flour
¼ cup confectioners' sugar

MACAROONS

These are used in lots of frozen and congealed desserts and are wonderful on their own, as well.

MAKES ABOUT 28 COOKIES.

Preparation

Preheat the oven to 350°. Work the almond paste and sugar together. Add egg whites. Sift together the flour and confectioners' sugar into the mix. Beat until smooth. Drop by spoonfuls onto a cookie sheet covered with parchment paper. Bake for 15 to 18 minutes, until light brown.

Ingredients

1   cup butter

1½   cups brown sugar

3   eggs

1   teaspoon baking soda

⅓   cup hot water

2   cups all-purpose flour

1   teaspoon ground cinnamon

½   teaspoon ground cloves

½   teaspoon ground allspice

½   teaspoon ground nutmeg

1   teaspoon salt

2   cups nuts

1   cup raisins

HERMITS

My grandmother's favorite cookie, chewy and full of spice. I found this recipe written down in a dozen places throughout her notes, always exactly the same. I think that she was trying to memorize it when her eyesight was failing.

MAKES ABOUT 3 DOZEN COOKIES.

Preparation

Preheat the oven to 350°. Grease a baking pan.

Cream together the butter and sugar. Beat in the eggs. Dissolve the soda in the hot water and stir in. Sift together the flour with the spices and salt and mix in, along with the nuts and raisins. Drop from a spoon onto the greased pan and bake for 15 minutes.

Ingredients

1½   cups sugar

2   eggs

½   cup shortening

½   cup butter, softened

2¾   cups all-purpose flour

2   teaspoons cream of tartar

1   teaspoon baking soda

¼   teaspoon salt

2   tablespoons sugar

2   teaspoons ground cinnamon

SNICKERDOODLES

These cookies make me smile just saying their name. All cookies smell good baking, but the aroma of cinnamon in Snickerdoodles could bring me inside on the sunniest day. Mama sent these to me at camp, in college, and even to culinary school in New York. I hid them under my bed and very rarely shared.

MAKES ABOUT 4 DOZEN COOKIES.

Preparation

Preheat the oven to 400°. Cream together 1½ cups of sugar and the eggs with shortening and butter. Sift the dry ingredients and mix in. Mix 2 tablespoons of sugar and the cinnamon together. Form small balls of the dough and roll in the cinnamon and sugar. Place on lightly greased cookie sheet and press down slightly. Bake for 10 minutes.

1   cup butter
1   cup sugar
2   eggs
2   teaspoons baking soda
2   tablespoons milk
2   teaspoons vanilla extract
2   teaspoons cream of tartar
3½ cups all-purpose flour
    Pinch salt

TEA CAKES

These are the cookie that we always used for decorating and icing, but they are also tasty made simply with no topping. Grandmother almost always had a tin of tea cakes in the pantry, or at least a log of dough in the ice box waiting to be made up.

To make these a little different, substitute rose or orange water for the vanilla.

MAKES ABOUT 4 DOZEN COOKIES.

Preparation

Cream the butter and sugar, and mix in the eggs. Dissolve the baking soda in the milk and add, along with the vanilla. Sift the dry ingredients together and stir in. Mix thoroughly. If you are going to roll and cut out cookies, gather the dough into a ball and wrap in plastic wrap. Alternately, roll the dough into a log and wrap in waxed paper. In either form, chill the dough for 15 minutes before proceeding. This makes the dough easier to handle.

Preheat the oven to 300°. Either slice ¼-inch circles from the log or roll out the ball of dough to ¼-inch thickness on a floured surface and cut out in desired shapes. Bake the tea cakes for about 20 minutes until golden brown. Any leftover dough will keep refrigerated for several days.

CRESCENT COOKIES

These are lovely, not too sweet cookies. Yummy with a cup of tea in the afternoon.

MAKES ABOUT 6 DOZEN COOKIES

Ingredients

- ½   cup butter
- ½   cup confectioners' sugar
- 2   teaspoons vanilla extract
- 2   cups all-purpose flour
- 1   cup finely chopped walnuts
      Additional confectioners' sugar

Preparation

Preheat the oven to 350°. Cream the butter and sugar and mix in the vanilla. Add the flour and walnuts and mix thoroughly. The dough will be very stiff. Shape by hand into crescents. Place on ungreased cookie sheet and bake for about 30 minutes.

Roll in confectioners' sugar while they are still warm.

OATMEAL COOKIES

This is from my great aunt Kate Brew Vaughn who taught and wrote cookbooks in the teens and twenties. I love the preserves in here. People know that they are there, but don't quite know what they are. A charming mystery.

MAKES ABOUT 3 DOZEN COOKIES.

Ingredients

- ½   cup shortening
- 1   cup brown sugar
- 2   eggs
- ½   cup strawberry preserves
- 1   tablespoon lemon juice
- 1   teaspoon ground cinnamon
- ½   teaspoon ground nutmeg
- ¼   teaspoon ground allspice
- 1   cup raisins
- ½   cup walnuts
- 1   cup rolled oats (not quick), steamed for 5 minutes
- 2   cups all-purpose flour
- ½   teaspoon baking powder
- 1   teaspoon salt

Preparation

Preheat the oven to 300°. Cream the shortening and sugar. Add eggs and beat well. Add the jam, lemon juice, spices, raisins, nuts, and steamed oats, and chill for 1 hour or so.

Sift together the flour, baking powder, and salt, and work into the dough. Drop on greased cookie sheet and bake for about 30 minutes.

Ingredients

- ³⁄₄ cup shortening
- 1 cup sugar
- 1 egg
- ³⁄₄ cup molasses
- 2 cups all-purpose flour
- 2 teaspoons baking soda
- 1 tablespoon ground ginger
- ½ teaspoon ground cinnamon
- ½ teaspoon salt
  Sugar for rolling

GINGERSNAPS

These taste like autumn to me. I like to eat them while they're still warm, with a cold glass of milk. Make certain that your ginger hasn't been sitting around in the cabinet for ages. Old ginger will lose its zing.

MAKES ABOUT 4 DOZEN COOKIES.

Preparation

Cream the shortening with the sugar. Beat in the egg and molasses. Sift the dry ingredients together over the wet mixture. Mix thoroughly. Form the dough into small balls and roll in the sugar. Place the cookies 2 inches apart on greased cookie sheet and bake at 350° for 10 to 15 minutes until the tops crack slightly and begin to brown. Remove the cookies from the pan while still warm and let cool on wire racks. Store in cookie tins.

Ingredients

- ½ cup firmly packed brown sugar
- ½ cup butter
- ½ cup light corn syrup
- ½ cup chopped pecans
- ¼ cup coconut
- 1 teaspoon vanilla extract

LACE COOKIES

A crunchy, candy-like little cookie, best served the day it's baked. Really nice with ice cream.

MAKES ABOUT 3 DOZEN COOKIES.

Preparation

Preheat the oven to 325°. Line a baking sheet with foil.

Bring the sugar, butter, and corn syrup to a boil on top of stove, stirring. Mix in remaining ingredients. Drop by teaspoonfuls onto the prepared pan and bake about 10 minutes, until lacy and brown at edges. Store on paper towels in a cookie tin.

6   egg whites
2   cups sugar
2   teaspoons vanilla extract
1   teaspoon vinegar

MERINGUE KISSES

This makes a dainty dessert for Valentine's Day or a little girl's birthday, especially served with peppermint ice cream. I also like them in the summer with a puddle of lemon curd and fresh berries scattered over.

MAKES ABOUT 3 DOZEN KISSES.

Preparation

Preheat the oven to 250°.

Beat the egg whites until stiff, but not dry. Beat in the sugar and fold in the vanilla and vinegar. Drop by tablespoon onto an ungreased baking sheet. Bake for 30 minutes. Reduce heat to 200° and bake another 30 minutes.

Remove from the oven and run a spatula under the cookies to avoid sticking.

Chapter 12

PIES AND COBBLERS

I think that pies are the most maternal of desserts. Surely this is some ingrained cultural nearsightedness on my part, yet one I can't erase. These exercises of rolling, cutting, crimping and baking. A fussiness not unlike a mother hen: that's how I am with pies, at least. I fuss over them. I worry with them. I fret about them while they bake. I pace while they are cooling, and then I beam while others remark on their goodness. Much like motherhood.

Ingredients

1½   cups all-purpose flour

1   teaspoon salt

¼   cup shortening

   Ice water just to catch dough,
      about 4 to 6 tablespoons

PIE CRUST

This is a great standard pie crust recipe. The shortening makes a flaky crust, and the seasoning works for any filling, sweet or savory. This one won't let you down.

FOR 1 PIE CRUST OR 6 3-INCH TARTS.

Preparation

Sift the flour with the salt. Mix the shortening in with your fingertips just until the mixture resembles cornmeal. Add just enough ice water to form a dough. Gather into a ball and place in the refrigerator for a few minutes before rolling out.

Ingredients

1   recipe pie crust
1   cup butter
2   cups sugar
4   eggs, separated
1   tablespoon cornstarch
2   tablespoons cream
    Pinch salt

CHESS PIE

There has been much speculation as to the origin of this peculiarly local mid-South dessert. The most likely answer, as with many things in these parts, is England, where a "Cheese Pie" is made from almost the identical recipe. Wherever it came from, Chess Pie is assuredly here to stay. They're at practically every church picnic or country cookout within a one-hundred-mile radius of Nashville. Simple, richly delicious, and travels well. Hard to improve upon that.

SERVES 6 TO 8.

Preparation

Roll out the pie crust and place in a pie pan. Refrigerate until filling is prepared.

Preheat the oven to 400°. Cream the butter and the sugar. Beat the egg yolks and add. Mix the cornstarch and cream into a paste and add, mixing well. Beat the egg whites with a pinch of salt until stiff and fold in. Pour into the prepared pie crust and bake at 400° for 5 minutes. Reduce the oven temperature to 375° and bake until the mixture sets and the crust is browned, about 30 minutes. Let cool and serve.

CHOCOLATE CHESS PIE

- 1   recipe pie crust
- 1½ squares unsweetened chocolate
- ½   cup butter
- 1   tablespoon all-purpose flour
- 1   cup firmly packed light brown sugar
- ½   cup sugar
- 2   eggs, beaten lightly
- 1   tablespoon milk
- 1   teaspoon vanilla extract

One more chess pie, this one to satisfy the chocoholic. I like to make individual tarts of all four kinds for larger parties or buffets.

SERVES 6 TO 8.

Preparation

Roll out the pie crust and line a 9-inch pie pan. Set in the refrigerator until the filling is prepared. Preheat the oven to 350°.

Melt the chocolate and butter in the top of a double boiler, stirring until smooth. Mix together the flour and sugars and add to the butter and chocolate. Mix well. Beat the eggs with the milk and vanilla. Add to the batter and beat by hand until smooth. Pour into pie crust and bake for 30 minutes. Let cool and serve.

LEMON CHESS PIE

- 1   recipe pie crust
- 4   eggs
- 1½ cups sugar
- 1   tablespoon cornstarch
- 1   tablespoon all-purpose flour
- ¼   teaspoon salt
-     Juice and grated rind of 2 lemons
- 1   cup butter, melted
- ½   cup evaporated milk

And yet another variation! This one is the zippiest.

SERVES 6 TO 8.

Preparation

Preheat the oven to 375°. Roll out pie crust dough and line a 9-inch pan. Refrigerate until filling is prepared.

Beat the eggs with the sugar. Combine the flour, salt, and cornstarch, and mix into the eggs. Add the juice and rind of the lemons. Mix in the melted butter and evaporated milk. Pour into the pie crust and bake about 30 minutes, until firm.

CARAMEL PIE

A beautiful, old-fashioned pie.

SERVES 6 TO 8.

Ingredients

- 1 recipe pie crust, rolled out in pie pan
- 3 eggs, separated
- ¾ cup plus ¾ cup sugar
- 2 tablespoons all-purpose flour
- 2 tablespoons butter
- Pinch salt
- 1½ cups milk
- 1 teaspoon vanilla extract

- 1 tablespoon white corn syrup
- 6 tablespoons sugar
- 1 teaspoon vanilla extract

Preparation

Preheat the oven to 375°. Line the pie crust with parchment paper and weigh down with beans or rice. Bake for 20 minutes.

Beat the egg yolks until light and fluffy. Add ¾ cup sugar, the flour, butter, salt, and milk. Mix well and cook in the top of a double boiler until lukewarm, stirring occasionally.

While the mixture is cooking, caramelize the remaining sugar in a heavy pan or iron skillet. With the caramel boiling, pour in the egg mixture, stirring constantly. Cook just until thickened. Remove from the heat and stir in the vanilla. Let the mixture cool while preparing the meringue.

Combine the corn syrup with the egg whites and beat until stiff. Gradually add the sugar and then the vanilla, beating until the whites hold in glossy peaks.

Preheat the oven to 300°. Pour the cooled caramel filling into the baked pie crust and spread the meringue over, working from the outside of the pie inwards. Bake for 20 minutes until the meringue is lightly browned.

BUTTERSCOTCH TARTS

- 1   recipe pie crust (page 195)
- 1   cup firmly packed dark brown sugar
- 3   tablespoons all-purpose flour
- ¼   teaspoon salt
- 1   cup milk, heated
- 5   eggs, separated
- 2   tablespoons butter
- 2   tablespoons sugar

MAKES ABOUT 5 TARTS.

Preparation

Preheat the oven to 350°. Spray the bottom of 5 4-inch tart shells with nonstick spray. Roll the dough out to about ⅟16 inch. Cut a circle about 5 to 6 inches in diameter. Ease the pastry into the tart shell, pressing into the corners and pinching the excess from the top of the shell. "Dock" the pastry by pricking the bottom with the tines of a fork. Place an empty shell directly over the crust. Repeat with the remaining dough. Bake for 15 to 20 minutes, until the edges begin to brown. Remove the top shell and continue baking until nicely browned, about 5 minutes more. Cool while you prepare the filling.

In a heavy, nonreactive saucepan mix the sugar, flour, and salt. Place over medium high heat and stir, melting the sugar as you would to make a caramel. Cook, stirring, until the sugar is melted and sandy. Carefully stir in the heated milk, as the mixture may splatter. Continue to cook, stirring, until the mixture is thickened, about 4 to 5 minutes. Remove from the stove.

In a small bowl whisk the egg yolks. Spoon a bit of the caramel into the yolks, whisking. Add another spoonful of caramel, then whisk the egg mixture back into the caramel. The yolks should thicken very quickly. If necessary, return the pan to the stove for a minute or two, stirring until thickened. Remove from the heat and stir in the cold butter. Pass the mixture through a sieve to catch any bits of coagulated egg. Refrigerate the filling for 30 minutes.

When the filling has cooled, prepare the meringue. Beat the egg whites to soft peaks. Add the sugar and beat until stiff, about 2 more minutes.

Pour the butterscotch into the baked pie crust. Top with meringue and bake at 350° until the meringue has browned, about 10 minutes. Cool before removing from the shells. Slide the tarts off the bottom round of the shell and serve.

½ cup butter

2½ squares unsweetened choco-
    late

2 eggs

1 cup sugar

¼ cup all-purpose flour

FUDGE PIE

Mama calls this her "emergency dessert" because she can make one up in under an hour. I just call it heaven.

SERVES 6 TO 8.

Preheat the oven to 350°. Grease a 9-inch pie pan. Melt the butter with the chocolate in the top of a double boiler. Let cool slightly. Beat the eggs with the sugar and flour, and mix into the chocolate. Pour into the prepared pie pan and bake for 30 minutes. Divine with peppermint ice cream.

1 recipe pie crust

6 tablespoons butter

1 cup plus 2 tablespoons sugar

3 eggs, separated

1 tablespoon cornstarch

3 tablespoons cream
   Juice and grated rind of 1
   lemon

LEMON MERINGUE PIE

This recipe was perfected by Catherine Couch, my grandmother's housekeeper and Mama's surrogate mother. Lemon Meringue Pie is just one reason we are all grateful to have been blessed with Couch.

SERVES 6 TO 8.

Preheat the oven to 350°. Roll out the pie crust and line a 9-inch pan. Crimp the edges with your finger and refrigerate while you prepare the filling.

Cream the butter and 1 cup sugar. Beat in the egg yolks. Mix the cornstarch into the cream and add. Stir in the lemon and rind. Pour into the prepared pie crust and bake on the lowest rack for 30 minutes, until set.

While the pie is baking, prepare the meringue. Beat the egg whites until soft peaks form. Add 2 tablespoons sugar and beat stiff.

Spread the meringue on the baked pie and return to the oven to brown, about 10 minutes.

1   recipe pie crust
3   eggs
½   cup sugar
1   cup dark Karo syrup
¼   teaspoon salt
1   teaspoon vanilla extract
2   cups chopped pecans

PECAN PIE

Perhaps the ultimate Southern pie, from Louisiana up through Virginia. Some pecan pies get quite elaborate with pralines, chocolate, or sweet potato layers. This one is straightforward pecans through and through. It holds well for picnics, or is good slightly heated with vanilla ice cream. Nice for individual tarts as well.

SERVES 6 TO 8.

Preheat the oven to 425°. Roll out the pie crust. Place in a pie pan, trimming and crimping the edges. Refrigerate while you prepare the filling.

Beat the eggs with the sugar. Add the syrup, salt, and vanilla, mixing well. Place the nuts in the bottom of the pie crust and pour the filling over. Bake on the bottom rack for 10 minutes. Reduce the heat to 350° and bake another 40 minutes, until set. Let cool and sprinkle with confectioners' sugar before serving.

1   recipe pie crust
1½ cups pecan halves
1   ounce semisweet baking
      chocolate
¼   cup butter
1   cup light corn syrup
½   cup sugar
2   teaspoons bourbon
¼   teaspoon salt
3   eggs

CHOCOLATE PECAN PIE

Adding a little interest for the chocolate lovers out there.

SERVES 6 TO 8.

Roll out pie crust dough and line a 9-inch pan. Place the pecan halves in the pie crust and refrigerate while preparing the filling.

Preheat the oven to 350°. Melt the chocolate and butter together in the top of a double boiler, stirring until smooth. Remove from heat and pour in the corn syrup and remaining ingredients, stirring well. Pour the mixture over the pecans in the pie crust and bake for about 1 hour, until set. Let cool before serving.

Ingredients

Juice of ½ lemon

8 small tart apples, peeled and thinly sliced, to make 5 cups (may substitute 4 Granny Smiths)

¾ cup sugar

1 tablespoon all-purpose flour

2 teaspoons ground cinnamon

¼ teaspoon salt

Grated rind of 1 lemon

2 recipes pie crust

2 tablespoons butter

1 egg, beaten with 2 tablespoons milk

APPLE PIE

This pie will warm anyone's heart. Try it with a bit of good Cheddar cheese.

SERVES 6 TO 8.

Preparation

Preheat the oven to 400°. Squeeze the lemon over the apples. Toss together and set aside.

Combine the sugar, flour, cinnamon, salt, and lemon rind in a bowl. Set aside.

Roll out half of the pie crust dough and line a 9-inch pan. Place the apples in the pie crust. Sprinkle the sugar mixture over apples. Dot with butter.

Roll out the remaining dough. Moisten the edges of the bottom pie crust and place top crust over. Flute the edges with your finger. Cut slits in the top crust and bake for 30 minutes. Remove the pie from the oven and brush lightly with the egg and milk, beaten together. Sprinkle with sugar. Return to the oven and bake another 10 minutes. Let cool to just warm before serving.

1   recipe pie crust

²/₃ cup firmly packed brown
      sugar

2   tablespoons all-purpose
      flour

1   teaspoon ground cinnamon

2   tablespoons butter

4   pounds fresh, ripe peaches
      Juice of ½ lemon

PEACH PIE

Only make this in the thick of summer, when the local peaches are luscious and juicy.

SERVES 6 TO 8.

Preparation

Preheat the oven to 375°. Roll out the dough to line a 9-inch pan, fluting the sides with your fingers. Set in the refrigerator while you prepare the filling.

Mix together the sugar, flour, and cinnamon. Work the butter in with your fingertips, making a crumb-like mixture.

Heat a large pot of water to boiling and prepare a bowl of ice water. Blanch the peaches for 2 minutes and plunge into the ice water. Peel and pit the peaches and cut into slices.

Remove the pie crust from the refrigerator and lay peach slices in a spiral in the pan, about half of the peaches. Sprinkle almost all of the crumb mixture over and arrange another spiral of peaches on top. Squeeze the lemon juice over this and sprinkle the remaining crumb mixture on top. Bake for 40 minutes and cool before slicing.

Ingredients

2   recipes pie crust

6   cups blackberries

⅔   cup sugar

    Grated zest of 2 lemons

2   teaspoons all-purpose flour

2   teaspoons butter

1   egg

¼   cup milk

BLACKBERRY PIE

A beautiful mid-summer dessert.

SERVES 6 TO 8.

Preparation

Preheat the oven to 375°. Roll out half of the pie crust dough and line a 10-inch pan, leaving a good inch of dough hanging over sides all around. Toss the blackberries with the sugar, lemon zest, and flour and place in the pie shell. Cut the butter in bits and dot the blackberries. Roll out the rest of the dough and cut in ¾-inch strips. Lay out in a lattice pattern over the pie. Trim the edges of the strips and pull up the overhanging dough, sealing the lattice and fluting the edge of the pie with your fingers. Mix the egg with the milk and use a pastry brush to apply to the crust. Sprinkle the top with sugar. Bake for 40 minutes, until the crust is browned and berries are bubbling. Cool before slicing.

Use the same recipe for cherry pie, stoning 2 quarts of cherries to get 6 cups of fruit.

FRIED FRUIT PIES

MAKES ABOUT 4 FRIED PIES FROM ONE RECIPE OF PIE CRUST DOUGH.

Preparation

I think that this was the first food that stood out in my mind as something special, something on a higher gustatory and spiritual level. Although I didn't put it like that when I was three years old, still, I knew.

You can make about four fried pies from one recipe of pie crust dough. Just toss some fresh fruit with sugar and a little lemon. Peaches, blackberries, and apples are all good choices.

Begin heating the oil in a deep fryer while you prepare the pies. Roll the dough out thin and cut in about 5-inch circles. Dip a fingertip in water and brush around the edge of the circle. Place 1 to 2 tablespoons of fruit in the center and fold the dough over, making a half moon. When the oil in the fryer reaches 325°, fry the pies for about 5 to 7 minutes, until the dough is crisp and nicely browned. Remove and drain well on clean brown paper bags. You may want to sprinkle confectioners' sugar over them. You may eat them right away, but at your own risk: the filling is hot and sticky!

Some people call these moon pies or sweetie pies. They're great to take on picnics, if you can get them that far without eating them all first.

SWEET POTATO PIE

Baking and mashing the sweet potatoes is the key step here. Lots of recipes tell you to boil the sweet potatoes, but you'll never get the rich flavor you get from baking the sweet potatoes in their skin. This is a wonderful autumn and winter dessert.

SERVES 6 TO 8.

Ingredients

1	recipe pie crust
3	sweet potatoes
1	cup butter, softened
1½	cups sugar
4	eggs
½	cup bourbon
	Grated rind and juice of ½ orange
1	teaspoon ground cinnamon

Preparation

Roll out the pie crust and line a 9-inch pan. Refrigerate while you prepare the filling.

Wash the sweet potatoes and bake for 30 minutes, until soft and squishy. Peel and mash. You need 2 cups mashed sweet potatoes. Save any extra for another use (babies love them!).

Preheat the oven to 425°. Cream the butter and sugar and mix with the potatoes. Add the eggs 1 at a time, blending well after each. Mix in the remaining ingredients. Pour the filling into the prepared pie shell and bake for 10 minutes. Turn the heat down to 350° and bake for 45 minutes, until the filling is set and the crust brown. Cool thoroughly and sift with confectioners' sugar just before serving. I like to use a 9-inch paper doily to sift the sugar through, making a pretty pattern on the pie.

Ingredients

2 eggs
1½ cups cooked pumpkin
1¼ cups milk
1 cup brown sugar
1 teaspoon cinnamon
1 tablespoon grated orange
   rind
1 teaspoon ground ginger
½ teaspoon fresh grated
   nutmeg
¼ teaspoon salt
1 recipe pie crust

PUMPKIN PIE

Canned pumpkin is perfectly good and saves you loads of time. Every once in a while, though, I think that it's nice to bake a pumpkin and scoop out and mash its flesh, as a fun project for children or just to remind yourself that Jack o'Lanterns are really a vegetable. If you do cook your own pumpkin, look for the yellower variety. They're generally meatier than the bright orange ones.

SERVES 6 TO 8.

Preparation

Preheat the oven to 475°. Beat the eggs into the pumpkin. Mix well with the remaining ingredients. Place in the top of a double boiler and cook until thickened. Pour into a prepared pie crust and place in the very hot oven. Reduce the heat to 300° after 5 minutes and cook until the crust is nicely browned.

Ingredients

1 recipe pie crust (for 6 tarts
   or one pie)

4 eggs, separated
2 cups sugar
1 cup pecans
1 cup raisins
1 teaspoon ground cinnamon
½ teaspoon ground cloves
3 tablespoons vinegar

OSGOOD PIES

These hold nicely for picnics and outings. They're very pretty, too.

MAKES 4 TARTS.

Preparation

Preheat the oven to 375 °. Roll out the pie crust and cut out in 6 circles to fit 4-inch tart pans. Refrigerate until ready to use.

Beat the yolks very well. Mix in everything but the egg whites. Separately beat the egg whites until frothy. Fold into the mixture. Pour into the prepared tart shells and bake until set.

MINCEMEAT FOR PIES

I will not deny that this is a bit of a production. This will, however, make enough mincemeat for several pies throughout the season. A jar of homemade mincemeat is a marvelous gift, quite rare in these modern times. Anyway, this production is a pleasant way to spend a gray or rainy Saturday, and think how wonderful your house will smell!

MAKES ABOUT 6 QUARTS. ONE QUART WILL GENEROUSLY FILL ONE PIE.

Ingredients

1	pound beef tongue
1½	pound round steak
2	pounds raisins
½	pound orange peel
2	pounds sugar
1	teaspoon ground allspice
1	teaspoon ground cloves
1	teaspoon ground cinnamon
1	teaspoon grated nutmeg
1	teaspoon white pepper
½	pound beef suet, chopped fine
	Zest and juice of 5 lemons
1	cup red wine
1	cup brandy
1½	cups cider

Preparation

Boil the tongue and round together in water to cover until tender. Drain and reserve the liquid. Let the meats cool and chop fine.

Cook the raisins, orange peel, and sugar in the liquid from the meat for thirty minutes. Drain and place in a large mixing bowl. Add the remaining ingredients. Put up and seal in quart jars. This will keep through the winter.

MINCEMEAT PIE

SERVES 6 TO 8.

Ingredients

2	recipes pie crust
1	quart mincemeat
1	egg
2	tablespoons milk
	Sugar

Preparation

Preheat the oven to 375°. Roll out half the pie crust dough and line a 9-inch pan. Fill with the mincemeat, adding a little water if it is too stiff. Roll out the remaining dough and cut in ½-inch-wide strips. Lay out over mincemeat in a lattice. Trim and crimp the edges. Stir together the egg and the milk and brush on the pastry. Sprinkle with sugar and bake for 40 minutes, until browned.

APPLE CRUMBLE

An easy year round bake. Really tasty.

SERVES 8.

Ingredients

15 small tart apples (or 7
      Granny Smiths), peeled,
      cored, and cut in eighths
   Juice and zest of 2 lemons
½ cup butter
½ cup firmly packed light
      brown sugar
½ cup plus ¼ cup sugar
1 cup all-purpose flour
½ teaspoon salt
1 teaspoon baking powder
2 eggs
1 teaspoon ground cinnamon
½ cup sliced almonds

Preparation

Preheat the oven to 350°. Butter an 8-inch square baking dish and set aside.

Toss the apples with the lemon juice. Set aside.

Cream together the butter, brown sugar, and ½ cup sugar. Sift the dry ingredients and mix into the butter. Beat in the eggs. Pour this into the baking dish. Arrange the apple slices on top of the batter. Mix the cinnamon with ¼ cup sugar. Sprinkle over the apples. Bake for 40 minutes.

Sprinkle the almond slices over the top and bake for 20 minutes more, until golden brown. Serve with vanilla ice cream.

STRAWBERRY RHUBARB CRISP

A nice tart, late spring dessert.

SERVES 8.

Ingredients

⅔ pound fresh strawberries
⅔ pound fresh rhubarb
   Juice of ½ lemon
¼ cup water
⅔ cup plus ⅓ cup sugar
¾ cup all-purpose flour
5 tablespoons butter
¾ cup firmly packed brown
      sugar

Preparation

Preheat the oven to 350°. Rinse and hull the strawberries. Slice in quarters and set aside.

Cut the rhubarb into 1-inch pieces. Place in a standard Pyrex baking dish and toss with lemon juice, water, and ⅔ cup sugar. Bake for 15 minutes. Add the strawberries and remaining sugar, tossing to evenly distribute in the pan.

Combine the flour, butter, and brown sugar into a crumb topping. Sprinkle over the fruit and bake for 15 more minutes, until nicely browned.

Ingredients

- 6 ripe peaches
- 1 pint blueberries
- ½ cup plus 2 tablespoons firm-ly packed brown sugar
- Juice of ½ lemon
- 2 tablespoons butter, cut in bits
- 1½ cups all-purpose flour
- 1½ teaspoons baking powder
- ½ teaspoon baking soda
- ¾ teaspoon salt
- 5 tablespoons butter
- 1 cup buttermilk
- 2 teaspoons sugar crystals

BISCUIT-TOPPED PEACH AND BLUEBERRY COBBLER

I like using different crusts for cobblers. This one is rich and very fast to make up, but it doesn't reheat really well. You can make the dough up ahead of time and have it sitting the fridge for a few hours. Drop it over the fruit right before you sit down and bake while you're having dinner. Perfect timing!

SERVES 6.

Preparation

Preheat the oven to 425°. Peel the peaches and slice directly into a baking dish. Toss with ½ cup brown sugar and lemon juice. Rinse and sort the blueberries and stir into the peaches. Dot with 2 tablespoons of butter and sprinkle with the remaining brown sugar. Set aside.

Sift the dry ingredients for the topping. Cut 5 tablespoons of butter into small bits and use just your fingertips to lightly work in the butter until the mixture resembles cornmeal. Pour in the buttermilk and mix together. Drop the dough by spoonfuls over the fruit. No need for symmetry. This looks beautiful slightly free form. Bake uncovered for 25 minutes.

Sprinkle the sugar crystals over and bake another 5 minutes, until the top is browned. Serve with whipped or clabbered cream, or with vanilla ice cream.

6   cups fresh blackberries
¾   cup plus 2 tablespoons sugar
¼   cup plus 2 tablespoons
    butter
1   recipe pie crust dough

BLACKBERRY COBBLER

A quintessential summer dessert. Certainly the easiest and perhaps most delicious way to deal with the buckets of blackberries we were always carrying home. The blackberries were usually ready to pick by the Fourth of July, and blackberry picking was at least a weekly activity for the following month. If you keep some pie crust handy in the fridge, you can have blackberry cobbler on the table in about an hour.

SERVES 8.

Preparation

Preheat the oven to 425°. Toss the blackberries with the sugar and place in a standard Pyrex baking dish. Cut ¼ cup of butter into bits and dot the top of the berries. Roll out the dough in a rough rectangle and cover the berries. Trim excess dough, but don't make it look too neat. Rustic looking cobblers are more appealing to me. Cut slits in the dough and bake for 20 minutes Pull the cobbler out of the oven and rub with 2 tablespoons butter and sprinkle with sugar. Return to the oven and bake for 20 more minutes, until the pastry is nicely browned and the filling is bubbly.

My mother adds 2 tablespoons of flour along with the berries and sugar. This thickens the juices somewhat. While I always use flour for a pie that must be cut, I'm not sure it's needed here. I like it either way.

This recipe is nice for a raspberry or mixed berry cobbler, also. Serve with ice cream or lightly sweetened whipped cream.

Chapter 13

ICE CREAM, PUDDINGS,
AND GOOEY STUFF

othing in the world tastes or feels like homemade ice cream. The creamy smooth richness that's just the right consistency, not frozen hard, like store bought. But I do worry that ice cream making has lost a little of its charm with all of the ease of modern machinery. There was a definite bonus in the anticipation and labor involved in hand-cranked ice cream freezers. Everyone wanted a turn to crank and prove their strength. The big boys and the Daddies were the last to crank. By that time everyone was gathered round, watching as the ice was pushed aside, the freezer drawn out, and the top lifted, then the paddle slowly pulled from the yummy, frozen mass. It's just different now that you pour the mixture into the freezer and set it on the countertop or in your refrigerator freezer, where the machine does all of the work while you watch TV. It's just not the same as being set up outside under a tree, in the midst of the badminton and croquet players. The ice cream tastes the same, I guess. But I sure do miss the dynamics of a hand-cranked ice cream party.

PEACH ICE CREAM

Ingredients

12 peaches, peeled and sliced
1½ cups superfine sugar
    Juice of 4 lemons
2 teaspoons vanilla extract
1 quart heavy cream

MAKES ABOUT 1½ QUARTS.

Preparation

Use a food processor to roughly purée the peaches with the sugar and lemon, leaving lots of little chunks of fruit. Place in a bowl and stir in the vanilla and cream.

Pour into an ice cream maker and freeze according to the manufacturer's directions.

STRAWBERRY ICE CREAM

Ingredients

1 quart strawberries
⅞ cup sugar
1 quart cream

Being a June baby, this was usually the ice cream made for my birthday. Even now I can't think of strawberry ice cream without seeing the neighborhood children wearing paper crowns and running through our green back yard that gave way to a creek and even greener woods. I can see the ice cream crank set up under the dogwood tree where my basset hound, Jubilation T. Cornpone, would be licking up the melting salted ice. Don't worry, he never got to the ice cream itself. Not until the guests were gone and he and I were alone.

MAKES 1½ QUARTS.

Preparation

Wash and hull the strawberries. Cut in pieces and place in a bowl, then pour the sugar over. Let sit for 1 hour, then press through a strainer, or purée in a food processor. Add the cream and freeze in an ice cream freezer according to the manufacturer's directions.

PEPPERMINT ICE CREAM

This is so good on top of hot fudge pie that I get goose bumps just thinking about it. Peppermint ice cream is also lovely and a bit more refined served with meringue puffs or kisses for Valentine's Day or for bride's maids' luncheons.

MAKES ABOUT 1 QUART.

Ingredients

- 6 ounces King Leo peppermint
- 2 cups whole milk
- 4 large egg yolks
- 1 cup superfine sugar
- 2 cups heavy cream, kept chilled

Preparation

Use a rolling pin to crack up the peppermint into small pieces. Set aside. Pour the milk in a saucepan and heat to simmering. Remove the pan from the heat. Heat the water in the bottom of a double boiler to simmering. Off the heat, place the egg yolks and sugar into the top of the double boiler and whisk together until pale yellow. Slowly pour in the hot milk, whisking. Place the top of the double boiler over the simmering (not boiling) water and cook, stirring constantly for 8 to 10 minutes, until the custard thickens enough to coat the back of a spoon. Remove from the heat and stir in the candy. Continue stirring until about two thirds of the candy is dissolved. Stir in the chilled cream. Refrigerate for 30 minutes.

Pour into an ice cream maker and freeze according to manufacturer's instructions.

Ingredients

1   loaf day old bread, cut in
    cubes
½   cup currants
4   large eggs
¾   cup plus 2 tablespoons sugar
4   cups milk
2   tablespoons vanilla extract
¼   teaspoon fresh grated
    nutmeg

BREAD PUDDING

What breathes reassurance better than this?

SERVES 8 OR MORE.

Preparation

Preheat the oven to 350°. Place the cubed bread in a 6-cup baking dish and toss the currants evenly over this. Beat the eggs and ¾ cup sugar together until light. Mix in the milk, vanilla, and nutmeg. Pour the mixture over the bread crumbs, trying to saturate all of the bread. Sprinkle the remaining sugar over the top. Fill a larger roasting pan halfway with simmering water and place the baking dish in the water bath. Place in the oven. Reduce the heat to 325° and bake for about 45 minutes, until set.

Let sit for 10 minutes before serving with whipped or ice cream, or Hard Sauce (recipe follows).

Ingredients

½   cup butter
2   cups confectioners' sugar
1   teaspoon vanilla extract
1   teaspoon whiskey

HARD SAUCE

Preparation

Cream together the butter and sugar. Whip until light and fluffy. Mix in the vanilla and whiskey. Keep chilled before serving. This is almost always served with plum pudding, as well.

3/4 cup rice

2 cups water

1 teaspoon salt

1/4 cup raisins

1 tablespoon whiskey

2 cups milk

4 eggs

1/2 cup sugar

1/2 teaspoon cinnamon

1/4 teaspoon mace

RICE PUDDING

SERVES 8.

Preparation

Grease a 1½-quart baking dish. Preheat the oven to 325°.

Place the rice, water, and salt together in a saucepan. Bring to a boil, stir, and cover. Turn the heat down to a simmer and cook for 15 minutes. Remove the lid and remove from the heat.

Place the raisins in a cup and pour the whiskey over. Set aside. Heat the milk in a saucepan to scalding. Remove from the heat and set aside.

Beat the eggs lightly with the sugar and add the raisins, spices, and rice. Slowly pour in the hot milk, stirring. Pour into the baking dish and bake for 1 hour. Test to see if the pudding is cooked through by inserting the blade of a knife. It should come out clean. If the pudding is set and the top not browned, set under the broiler for a few minutes. Serve warm.

Ingredients

1 dozen oranges, peeled and sliced

1 pineapple, cut in cubes

1 large coconut, grated

1 cup sugar

AMBROSIA

Tropical fruit was a great luxury before air-freight and overnight express. Ambrosia was served at only the most special times, usually around Christmas.

SERVES 12.

Preparation

In a bowl or casserole, layer the orange, pineapple, and coconut until the dish is full, having coconut on the last layer. Sprinkle with sugar. Refrigerate for 2 hours before serving.

2 tablespoons gelatin

½ cup cold water

¼ cup milk

1 quart heavy whipping cream

4 egg whites

⅔ pound confectioners' sugar
(or less)

2 teaspoons vanilla extract

6 macaroons, broken in pieces

2 dozen lady fingers

¼ cup pecans

¼ cup candied cherries (red
and green)

CHARLOTTE RUSSE

This has always been the Christmas dinner dessert in my family. My great-great grandmother recorded a recipe for it in her notebook in 1865. Rich, white, very sweet, and very fluffy. I thought that this was what the angels had for dessert every day. We were lucky enough to get it at Christmas.

SERVES ABOUT 12 TO 16.

Preparation

Soak the gelatin in the water. Heat in the top of a double boiler over simmering water to completely dissolve. Remove from heat, stir in the milk, and cool to lukewarm.

Whip the cream and and add the gelatin mixture, beating all the time.

Beat the egg whites until almost stiff. Add the sugar and vanilla, and beat stiff. Fold into the cream mixture. Fold in three-fourths of the broken macaroons. Line a bowl or bowls with the ladyfingers. Spoon in the cream mixture. Decorate the top with the remaining macaroons, pecans, and cherries.

Chapter 14

BEVERAGES

❧

The beverages we drink are frequently lost to us today, hiding in Styrofoam or plastic cups and slurped through a straw, they are never even seen. Such a pity, because drinks can be as refreshing visually as they are to our parched throats. Served in a pretty, tall glass over ice, garnished with citrus, flowers, or herbs, such fun to hold and turn, catch the falling beads. Think about sitting on the porch in a comfortable chair, taking a few moments to slow down, relax; enjoy the scenery; your home; your family; your beautiful, frosty glass of iced tea. This is, after all, what you're working so hard for.

Ingredients

1   generous bunch of mint
1   quart boiling water
2   large tea bags meant for
      iced tea, such as Tetley
2   cup sugar
     Juice of 4 lemons
     Juice of 4 oranges
     Water to make 1 gallon

TEA PUNCH

Every tearoom has its own version of this fruited tea. This one's not too sweet.

MAKES 1 GALLON.

Preparation

Place the mint in a large pitcher and pour the boiling water over. Add the tea bags and sugar. Let steep for ten minutes. Remove the mint and tea bags. Add the juices and water to make 1 gallon. Serve over ice with mint and a thin lemon circle for garnish.

Ingredients

2   quarts blackberries
1   pound sugar
¼   teaspoon ground mace
½   teaspoon ground ginger
¼   teaspoon ground allspice
6   whole cloves
3   sticks cinnamon
1   cup brandy or bourbon

BLACKBERRY CORDIAL

Cordial indeed. This dainty little beverage packs a kick.

MAKES A LITTLE OVER 1 QUART.

Preparation

Purée the blackberries and strain to obtain 1 quart of juice. Place in a saucepan with the sugar and spices and bring to a boil. Skim and let cool. Add the brandy. Bottle and seal.

BLACKBERRY OR RASPBERRY VINEGAR

This is the most delightful drink I can imagine on a muggy August day.

MAKES 1 QUART SWEET VINEGAR.

2 quarts berries
1 quart cider vinegar
1 scant cup sugar

Sparkling water
Fresh berries
Lemon and lime wedges

Preparation

Pick over the berries and place in a glass or ceramic bowl. Pour in the vinegar. Let stand for 24 hours and strain into a saucepan. Add the sugar and boil for thirty minutes. Cool, bottle and cork tightly. To serve, use half vinegar to half sparkling water. Garnish with lemon and lime.

BLACKBERRY WINE

Nice for dessert, a delightful Christmas present.

MAKES ABOUT 1½ QUARTS.

Ingredients

1 gallon blackberries
1 quart boiling water
2 pounds sugar

Preparation

Place the berries in a large bowl and bruise slightly by pressing. Pour the boiling water over. Let that stand for twenty-four hours, stirring occasionally. Strain off the liquid into a cask or jug. Add the sugar, stir, and cork. Let stand for three months, then bottle and cork.

Ingredients

4   lemons
3   tablespoons sugar or to taste
32   ounces cold water

LEMONADE

Custom made for front porches, back porches, and the shade of your favorite tree.

FOR 4 TALL GLASSES.

Preparation

Halve and juice the lemons and stir in the sugar to dissolve. Add the water and taste to see if you want more sugar. Pour over cracked ice and garnish with thin lemon circles.

Ingredients

1   gallon milk
16   egg yolks
2   cups sugar
1   tablespoon vanilla extract
Whole nutmeg

BOILED CUSTARD

Is it a dessert or a beverage? I'm not sure, but it sure is mighty tasty. Warms things up at Christmastime.

MAKES A LITTLE OVER 1 GALLON.

Preparation

Place the milk in a large, heavy saucepan over medium heat. Do not boil. Beat the yolks with the sugar and ladle in some of the hot milk, stirring constantly. Stir this into the saucepan and heat, stirring for about 20 minutes, until the custard coats the back of a spoon. The custard should reach 190°.

Remove the pan from the stove and place in a sink half filled with cold water to cool the custard quickly. Serve in cups with nutmeg grated over.

INDEX

A

Ambrosia, 215
Angel Food Cake, 181
apples
    Apple and Walnut Salad with Blue Cheese
      Dressing, 43
    Apple Breakfast Cake, 163
    Apple Crumble, 208
    Apple Pie, 202
    Southern Fried Apples, 143
asparagus, 48-50
Aspic, Tomato, 36

B

Baked Beans, 51
Baked Rice, 89
Baked Sweet Potatoes, 94
Banana Bread with Black Walnuts, 168
barbecue
    Barbecued Pork Shoulder, 146
    Chicken Piquant for Barbecue, 125
    Red Barbecue Sauce, 147
    Vinegar Barbecue Sauce, 147
Batter Bread, 158
beans
    Baked Beans, 51
    Butter Beans, 54
    Country-style Green Beans, 52
    Creamy White Bean Soup, 27
    Fresh October Bean Soup, 25
    Fresh Three Bean Salad, 39
    Green Beans with Chili Sauce, 52
    Lima Bean Croquettes, 105
    Lima Bean Salad, 37
    October Beans, 55
    Summer Green Beans with Herbs, 53
    White Bean Croquettes, 106
Beaten Biscuits, 19
beef
    Beef Stew, 140
    Meat Pie, 139
    Meat Loaf, 138
    Pot Roast, 137
    Spiced Round, 141
    Vegetable Beef Soup, 30
beets, 40-41
Beverages, 217-220
Biscuit Dumplings, 122
biscuits
    Beaten Biscuits, 19
    Buttermilk Biscuits, 160
    Cinnamon Biscuit Scraps, 161
    Marmalade Cheese Pastries, 18
    Sweet Potato Biscuits, 161
    Whole Wheat Biscuits, 159
Biscuit-topped Peach and Blueberry Cobbler, 209
blackberries
    Blackberry Cobbler, 210
    Blackberry Cordial, 218
    Blackberry Jam, 10
    Blackberry Jam Cake, 179
    Blackberry or Raspberry Vinegar, 219
    Blackberry Pie, 204

Blackberry Wine, 219
black-eyed peas
    Black-Eyed Pea Salad, 38
    Black-Eyed Peas (Hoppin' John), 57
    Dried Black-Eyed Pea Soup, 26
Blueberry Cobbler, Biscuit-topped Peach and, 209
Blue Cheese Dressing, 43
Boiled Cabbage with Butter, 59
Boiled Custard, 220
Boiled Shrimp, 114
Boiled Turnips Browned in Butter, 102
Boiled White Icing, 176
Braised Red Cabbage, 59
Bread and Butter Pickles, 6
Bread Pudding, 214
Breads, 151-170
Breakfast Cake, Apple, 163
Breakfast Sausage, 150
Broiled Tomatoes, 97
Brown Gravy for Meat Loaf, 138
Brownies, Butterscotch, 184
Brunswick Stew, 129
Brussels sprouts
    Brussels Sprouts with Brown Butter, 58
    Marinated Brussels Sprouts, 42
Buns, Hot Cross, 167
Butter Beans, 54
Buttered Parsnips, 79
buttermilk
    Buttermilk Biscuits, 160
    Buttermilk Corn Bread, 155
    Buttermilk Griddle Cakes, 156
    Cold Squash and Buttermilk Soup, 27
Butterscotch Brownies, 184
Butterscotch Tarts, 199

C

cabbage
    Boiled Cabbage with Butter, 59
    Braised Red Cabbage, 59
    Cabbage Pickle, 8

Cabbage Soup with Root Vegetables, 29
    Chow Chow, 5
    Cole Slaw, 35
    Crowder Pea and Cabbage Stew, 56
    Stuffed Cabbage, 60
    Vegetable Beef Soup, 30
Cakes and Cookies, 171-194
candies, 185-188
caramel
    Caramel Apples, 186
    Caramel Cake, 176
    Caramel Icing, 177
    Caramel Pie, 198
carrots
    Copper Penny Carrots, 61
    Peas and Carrots with Cream, 82
Catfish, Fried, 118
Charlotte Russe, 216
Cheddar
    Cheese Soufflé, 63
    Cheese Straws, 16
    Macaroni and Cheese, 62
    Marmalade Cheese Pastries, 18
    Pimiento Cheese, 17
    Squash Casserole, 94
cheese, see also Cheddar
    Apple and Walnut Salad with Blue Cheese
        Dressing, 43
    Asparagus Gratin, 50
    Blue Cheese Dressing, 43
    Cheese Grits, 67
    Flower Sandwiches, 18
    Ginger Date Nut Bread with Cream Cheese, 17
    Olives, Dates or Almonds in Cheese Pastry, 19
    Patty Pan Squash with Cheese Grits, 93
    Tomatoes Stuffed with Herbed Rice, 99
    Watercress Sandwiches, 14
Chess Pie, 196
chicken, 120-129
    Chicken and Rice Soup, 31
    Chicken Salad, 45

Chicken-fried Steak, 136

Chicken Gravy, 121

Chili Sauce, 4

chocolate
    Chocolate Chess Pie, 197
    Chocolate Icing, 175
    Chocolate Pecan Pie, 201
    Fudge Cake, 177
    Fudge Pie, 200
    Toll House Cookies, 186

Chow Chow, 5

Cinnamon Biscuit Scraps, 161

cobblers, 209-210

Cocktail Sauce, 115

Coconut Icing, 174

Cold Cucumber Sandwiches, 12

Cold Squash and Buttermilk Soup, 27

Cold Tomato Soup with Cucumber and Mint, 28

Cole Slaw, 35

Conserve, Pear and Ginger, 10

cookies, 188-194

Copper Penny Carrots, 61

corn, 64-66
    Fresh Corn Batter Cakes, 155
    Tomatoes with Corn, 100

corn bread, 152-158

Corn Bread Stuffing, 131

Corn Fritters, 104

Corn Light Bread, 154

Cornmeal Waffles, 162

Corn Pones, 152

Corn Pudding with Sage, 65

Cottage Fries, 86

country ham, 148-149

Country Ham Sandwiches, 15

Country Ham Steaks with Red Eye Gravy, 149

Country Squash, 91

Country-style Green Beans, 52

Crackling Pones, 156

Cranberry Loaf, 169

Creamed Chicken, 127

Creamy White Bean Soup, 27

Creole Shrimp-stuffed Peppers, 83

Crescent Cookies, 192

Crisp, Strawberry Rhubarb, 208

croquettes
    Chicken Croquettes, 128
    Lima Bean Croquettes, 105
    Rice Croquettes, 107
    Sweet Potato Croquettes, 107
    White Bean Croquettes, 106

Crowder Pea and Cabbage Stew, 56

Crumble, Apple, 208

cucumbers
    Bread and Butter Pickles, 6
    Cold Cucumber Sandwiches, 12
    Cold Tomato Soup with Cucumber and Mint, 28
    Mustard Pickle, 7
    Tomato and Cucumber Salad, 35

Custard, Boiled, 220

D

dates
    Ginger Date Nut Bread, 167
    Ginger Date Nut Bread with Cream Cheese, 17
    Olives, Dates or Almonds in Cheese Pastry, 19

Deep-fried Frog's Legs, 113

Deep-fried Oysters, 112

Deep-fried Shrimp, 115

Dill Pickles, 6

Divinity Fudge, 185

Dried Black-Eyed Pea Soup, 26

Dumplings, Biscuit, 122

E

eggplant, 70-71

Egg Salad, 34

Eggs, Stuffed, 22

F

Flower Sandwiches, 18

French Dressing, True, 41
Fresh Corn Batter Cakes, 155
Fresh October Bean Soup, 25
Fresh Peas with Butter and Mint, 81
Fresh Three Bean Salad, 39
Fried Brook Trout, 116
Fried Catfish, 118
Fried Calf's Liver, 137
Fried Chicken, 120
Fried Corn, 64
Fried Eggplant, 71
Fried Fruit Pies, 205
Fried Green Tomatoes, 98
Fried Livers and Gizzards, 121
Fried Okra, 74
Fried Sweet Potatoes, 95
Fries, Cottage, 86
Fritters and Little Fried Things, 103-108
Frog's Legs, Deep-fried, 113
Fruit Cake, 183
fudge
    Divinity Fudge, 185
    Fudge Cake, 179
    Fudge Pie, 200
    Peanut Butter Fudge, 185

G

Garlic Mashed Potatoes, 85
Giblet Gravy, 132
ginger
    Ginger Cake, 175
    Ginger Date Nut Bread, 167
    Ginger Date Nut Bread with Cream Cheese, 17
    Ginger Snaps, 193
Gizzards, Fried Livers and, 121
Glazed Country Ham, 149
Glazed Onions, 76
goat cheese
    Asparagus Gratin, 50
    Flower Sandwiches, 18
    Tomatoes Stuffed with Herbed Rice, 99

Watercress Sandwiches, 14
Grandmama's Pineapple Cake, 178
Grandmama's White Bread, 156
gravy
    Brown Gravy for Meat Loaf, 138
    Chicken Gravy, 121
    Country Ham Steaks with Red Eye Gravy, 149
    Giblet Gravy, 132
    Sausage Gravy, 150
green beans, 52-53
greens, 72-73
griddle cakes
    Buttermilk Griddle Cakes, 156
    Fresh Corn Batter Cakes, 155
    Squash Griddle Cakes, 157
grits
    Cheese Grits, 67
    Patty Pan Squash with Cheese Grits, 93
    Simple Grits, 67

H

ham
    Country Ham Steaks with Red Eye Gravy, 149
    Country Ham Sandwiches, 15
    To Cook A Country Ham, 148
Hard Sauce, 214
Hash, Turkey, 132
Hermits, 190
Hominy, Seasoned, 68
Honey Whole Wheat Bread, 164
Hot Cross Buns, 167
Hot Water Corn Bread, 153
Hush Puppies, 108

I

Ice Cream, Puddings, and Gooey Stuff, 211-216
icing
    Boiled White Icing, 176
    Caramel Icing, 177
    Chocolate Icing, 175
    Coconut Icing, 174

Strawberry Icing, 174
Pineapple Icing, 178

J

jam
Blackberry Jam, 10
Peach Jam, 9
Rhubarb Jam, 9
Johnny Cake, 158

K

Ketchup, Tomato, 4

L

Lace Cookies, 193
Lamb, Roast, 142
lemon
Lemonade, 220
Lemon Chess Pie, 197
Lemon Meringue Pie, 200
Lemon Squares, 184
Lemon Tea Bread, 170
lima beans
Lima Bean Croquettes, 105
Lima Bean Salad, 37
Succotash, 32
liver
Fried Calf's Liver, 137
Fried Livers and Gizzards, 121

M

Macaroni and Cheese, 62
Macaroons, 189
Marinated Asparagus, 49
Marinated Brussels Sprouts, 42
Marinated Shrimp Salad, 46
Marmalade Cheese Pastries, 18
Mary Mell Clement's Sugar Cookies, 189
mashed potatoes, 84-85
Mashed Sweet Potatoes, 96
Mayonnaise, 14

Meat Loaf, 138
Meat Pie, 139
Meats, 135-150
Meringue Kisses, 194
Mincemeat for Pies, 207
Mincemeat Pie, 207
mint
Cold Tomato Soup with Cucumber and Mint, 28
Fresh Peas with Butter and Mint, 81
Marinated Asparagus, 49
Tea Punch, 218
Tomato and Cucumber Salad, 35
Tomatoes Stuffed with Herbed Rice, 99
Mustard Pickle, 7

O

Oatmeal Cookies, 192
October beans
Fresh October Bean Soup, 25
October Beans, 55
okra
Fried Okra, 74
Stewed Okra, 75
Old-fashioned Greens, 72
Olives, Dates or Almonds in Cheese Pastry, 19
1-2-3-4 Cake, 173
onions
Glazed Onions, 76
Onion Rings, 78
Onion Soufflé, 77
Scalloped Onions, 76
Open-Face Tomato Sandwiches, 13
Orange Candied Pecans, 187
Osgood Pies, 206
oysters
Deep Fried Oysters, 112
Oyster Stew, 111
Scalloped Oysters, 110

P

Pan-baked Rabbit, 134

Pan-fried Pork Chops, 145
Pancakes, Potato, 87
Pantry, The, 3-10
Parsnip Balls, 104
parsnips, 79-80
Patty Pan Squash with Cheese Grits, 93
peaches
    Biscuit-topped Peach and Blueberry Cobbler, 209
    Peach Ice Cream, 212
    Peach Jam, 9
    Peach Pie, 203
    Spiced Peaches, 8
Peanut Brittle, 186
Peanut Butter Fudge, 185
Pear and Ginger Conserve, 10
peas, 81-82
    Black-Eyed Pea Salad, 38
    Crowder Pea and Cabbage Stew, 56
    Dried Black-Eyed Pea Soup, 26
Pecan Pie, 201
Pecans, Orange Candied, 187
Peppermint Ice Cream, 213
Peppers, Creole Shrimp-stuffed, 83
Pickled Beet Salad, 41
pickles
    Bread and Butter Pickles, 6
    Cabbage Pickle, 8
    Dill Pickles, 6
    Mustard Pickle, 7
    Watermelon Pickle, 5
Pie Crust, 195
Pies and Cobblers, 195-210
Pimiento Cheese, 17
Pineapple Icing, 178
Pinwheels, Sausage, 15
Poke Salet, 73
pones
    Corn Pones, 152
    Crackling Pones, 156
    Sweet Potato Pones, 153
Popcorn Balls, 187

Popovers, 159
Poppy Seed Dressing for Fruit Salad, 44
pork
    Barbecued Pork Shoulder, 146
    Country Ham Sandwiches, 15
    Country Ham Steaks with Red Eye Gravy, 149
    Pan-fried Pork Chops, 145
    Slow Baked Pork Chops, 144
    To Cook A Country Ham, 148
potatoes, 84-88
    Baked Sweet Potatoes, 94
    Beet and New Potato Salad, 40
    Fried Sweet Potatoes, 95
    Mashed Sweet Potatoes, 96
    Potato Salad, 34
    Roasted Sweet Potatoes, 95
    Sweet Potato Biscuits, 161
    Sweet Potato Pie, 206
    Sweet Potato Pones, 153
    Sweet Potato Croquettes, 107
Pot Pie, Chicken, 124
Pot Roast, 137
Poultry, 119-134
Pound Cake, 182
Pralines, 188
pudding
    Bread Pudding, 214
    Corn Pudding with Sage, 65
    Rice Pudding, 215
pumpkin
    Pumpkin Bread, 170
    Pumpkin Pie, 206
Punch, Tea, 218

Q

Quail, Roast, with Bacon, 133

R

Rabbit, Pan-baked, 134
Raspberry Vinegar, Blackberry or, 219
Red Barbecue Sauce, 147

Red Eye Gravy, Country Ham Steaks with, 149
Rhubarb Jam, 9
rice
    Baked Rice, 89
    Chicken and Rice Soup, 31
    Chicken Baked in Rice, 123
    Rice, 89
    Rice Croquettes, 107
    Rice Pudding, 215
    Tomatoes Stuffed with Herbed Rice, 99
Roast Chicken, 126
Roasted or Grilled Corn, 66
Roasted New Potatoes, 88
Roasted Sweet Potatoes, 95
Roast Lamb, 142
Roast Quail with Bacon, 133
Roast Turkey with Cornbread Stuffing, 130
Rolls, Yeast, 166

S

sage
    Breakfast Sausage, 150
    Corn Bread Stuffing, 131
    Corn Pudding with Sage, 65
    Meat Loaf, 138
    Onion Soufflé, 77
    Patty Pan Squash with Cheese Grits, 93
    Stuffed Cabbage, 60
salad dressings
    Blue Cheese Dressing, 43
    Mayonnaise, 14
    Poppy Seed Dressing for Fruit Salad, 44
    True French Dressing, 41
Salads, 33-48
Salmon Balls, 117
Salsify, 90
sandwiches
    Cold Cucumber Sandwiches, 12
    Country Ham Sandwiches, 15
    Flower Sandwiches, 18
    Ginger Date Nut Bread with Cream Cheese, 17
    Open-Face Tomato Sandwiches, 13
    Thanksgiving Night Turkey Sandwich, 131
    Watercress Sandwiches, 14
sauces
    Chili Sauce, 4
    Cocktail Sauce, 115
    Hard Sauce, 214
    Red Barbecue Sauce, 147
    Tartar Sauce, 112
    Tomato Sauce, 113
    Vinegar Barbecue Sauce, 147
sausage
    Breakfast Sausage, 150
    Sausage Pinwheels, 15
Sausage Gravy, 150
Sautéed Cucumber, 69
Scalloped Onions, 76
Scalloped Oysters, 110
Scalloped Parsnips, 80
Scalloped Potatoes, 86
Seafood, 109-118
Seasoned Hominy, 68
Shortcake, Strawberry, 180
shrimp, 114-115
    Creole Shrimp-stuffed Peppers, 83
    Marinated Shrimp Salad, 46
Simple Asparagus, 48
Simple Grits, 67
slaw, Cole Slaw, 35
Slow Baked Pork Chops, 144
Snacks, 11-22
Snickerdoodles, 190
Soups, 23-32
Southern Fried Apples, 143
Spice Cake, 177
Spiced Peaches, 8
Spiced Round, 141
Spoon Bread, 154
squash, 91-95
    Cold Squash and Buttermilk Soup, 27
    Squash Griddle Cakes, 157

Steamed Summer Squash, 92
stew
    Beef Stew, 140
    Brunswick Stew, 129
    Crowder Pea and Cabbage Stew, 56
    Oyster Stew, 111
Stewed Eggplant, 70
Stewed Okra, 75
Stewed Tomatoes, 101
strawberries
    Strawberry Bread, 168
    Strawberry Ice Cream, 212
    Strawberry Icing, 174
    Strawberry Rhubarb Crisp, 208
    Strawberry Shortcake, 180
Stuffed Cabbage, 60
Stuffed Eggs, 22
Stuffing, Corn Bread, 131
Succotash, 32
Sugar Cookies, Mary Mell Clement's, 189
Summer Green Beans with Herbs, 53
sweet potatoes, 94-96
    Sweet Potato Biscuits, 161
    Sweet Potato Croquettes, 107
    Sweet Potato Pie, 206
    Sweet Potato Pones, 153

T

Tartar Sauce, 112
Tea Cakes, 191
Tea Punch, 218
Thanksgiving Night Turkey Sandwich, 131
To Cook A Country Ham, 148
Toll House Cookies, 189
tomatoes, 97-101
    Chili Sauce, 4

Cold Tomato Soup with Cucumber and Mint, 28
Greens with Tomatoes, 73
Mustard Pickle, 7
Open-Face Tomato Sandwiches, 13
Tomato and Cucumber Salad, 35
Tomato Aspic, 36
Tomato Ketchup, 4
Tomato Sauce, 113
Trout, Fried Brook, 116
True French Dressing, 41
turkey, 130-132
Turnips, Boiled, Browned in Butter, 102

V

Vegetable Beef Soup, 30
Vegetables and Sides, 47-102
Vinegar Barbecue Sauce, 147
Vinegar, Blackberry or Raspberry, 219

W

Waffles, 162
Watercress Sandwiches, 14
Watermelon Pickle, 5
White Bread, Grandmama's, 156
white beans
    Creamy White Bean Soup, 27
    White Bean Croquettes, 106
whole wheat
    Honey Whole Wheat Bread, 164
    Whole Wheat Biscuits, 159
Wine, Blackberry, 219

Y

Yeast Rolls, 166